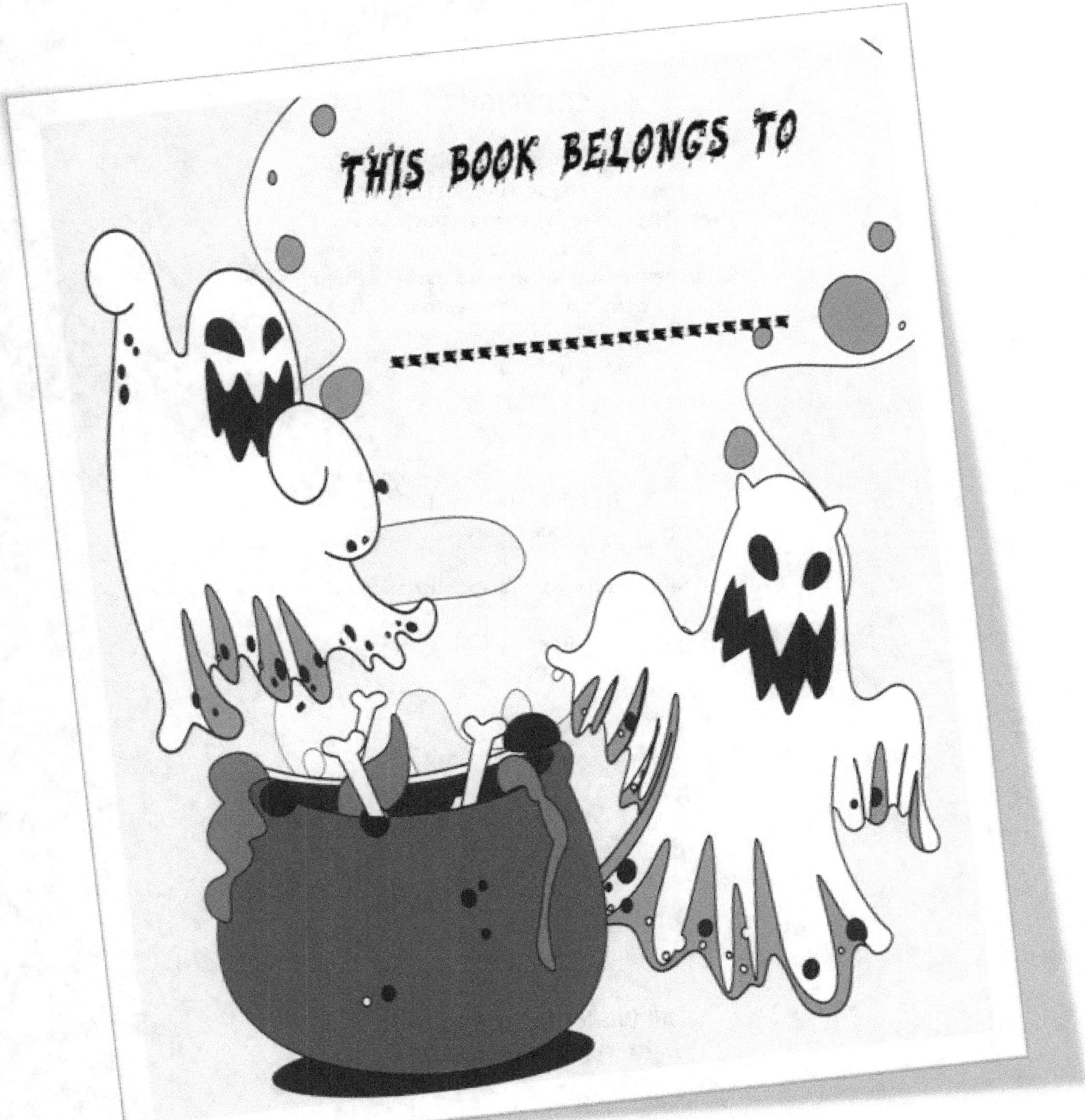

COPYRIGHT

The transmission, duplication, or reproduction of this entire book or any portion may not be used in any manner whatsoever without the expressed written permission of the author.

First Published in 2020
Faith Martin

faith.martin@arcadiapublisher.co.uk

Reading (UK)

**All World Rights Reserved
© Faith Martin 2020**

Recommendation

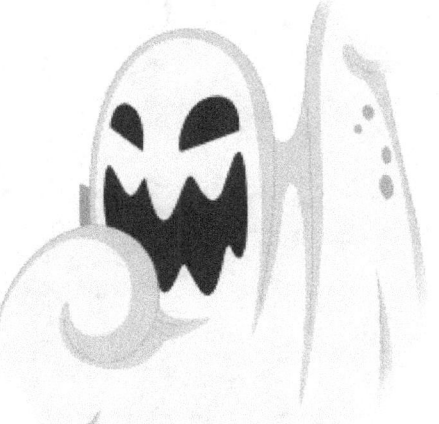

In order to fully enjoy this book we recommend to you first points:

1) That you do not use water media to colour these picture as it may bleed through the page and soil the image below.

   The quality of the paper this book is printed on, is beyond are control.

2) That in order to protect future images after the one you are working on, that you place a small pice of cardboard between it and the next.

With that say, enjoy colouring these

HALLOWEEN IMAGES......

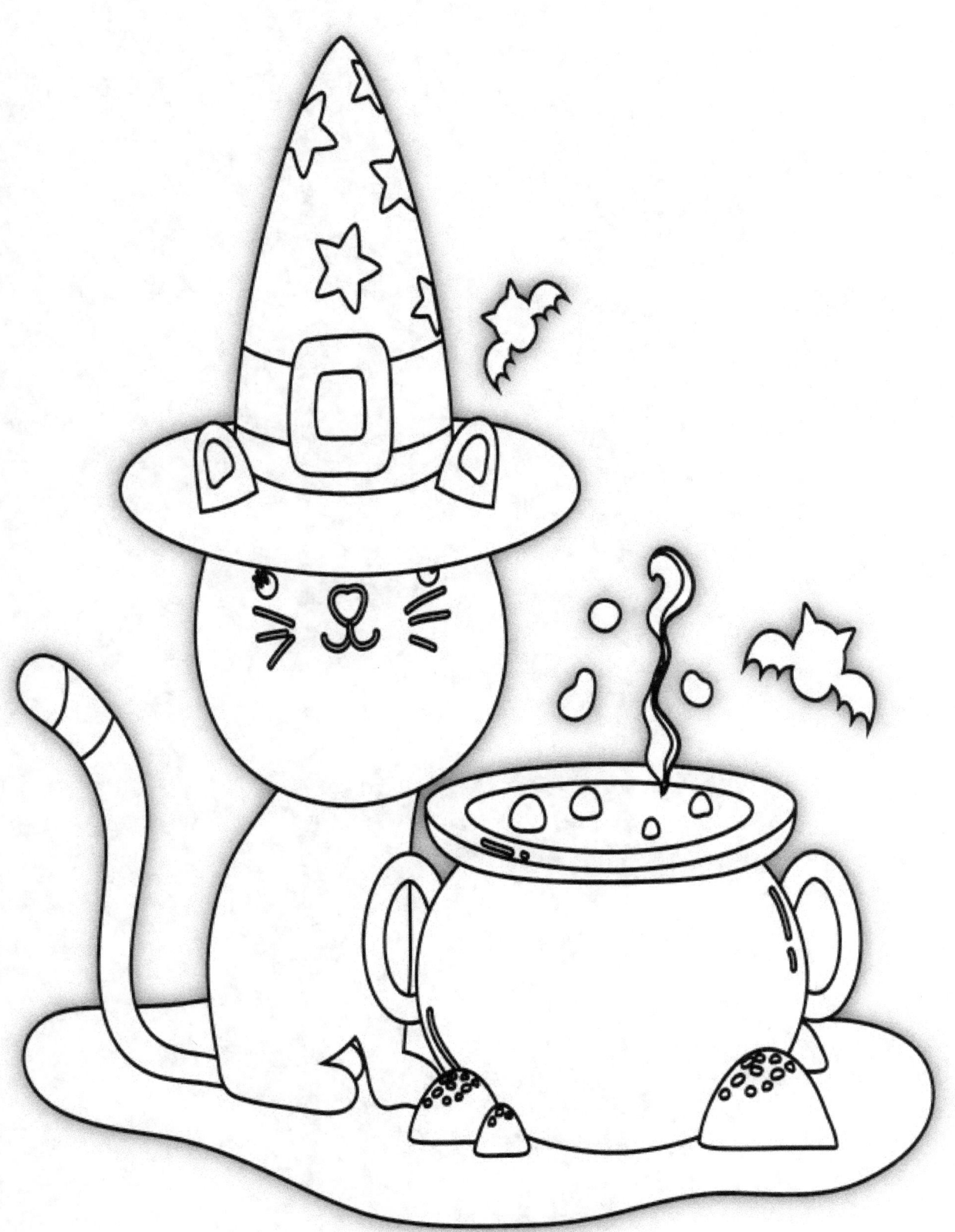

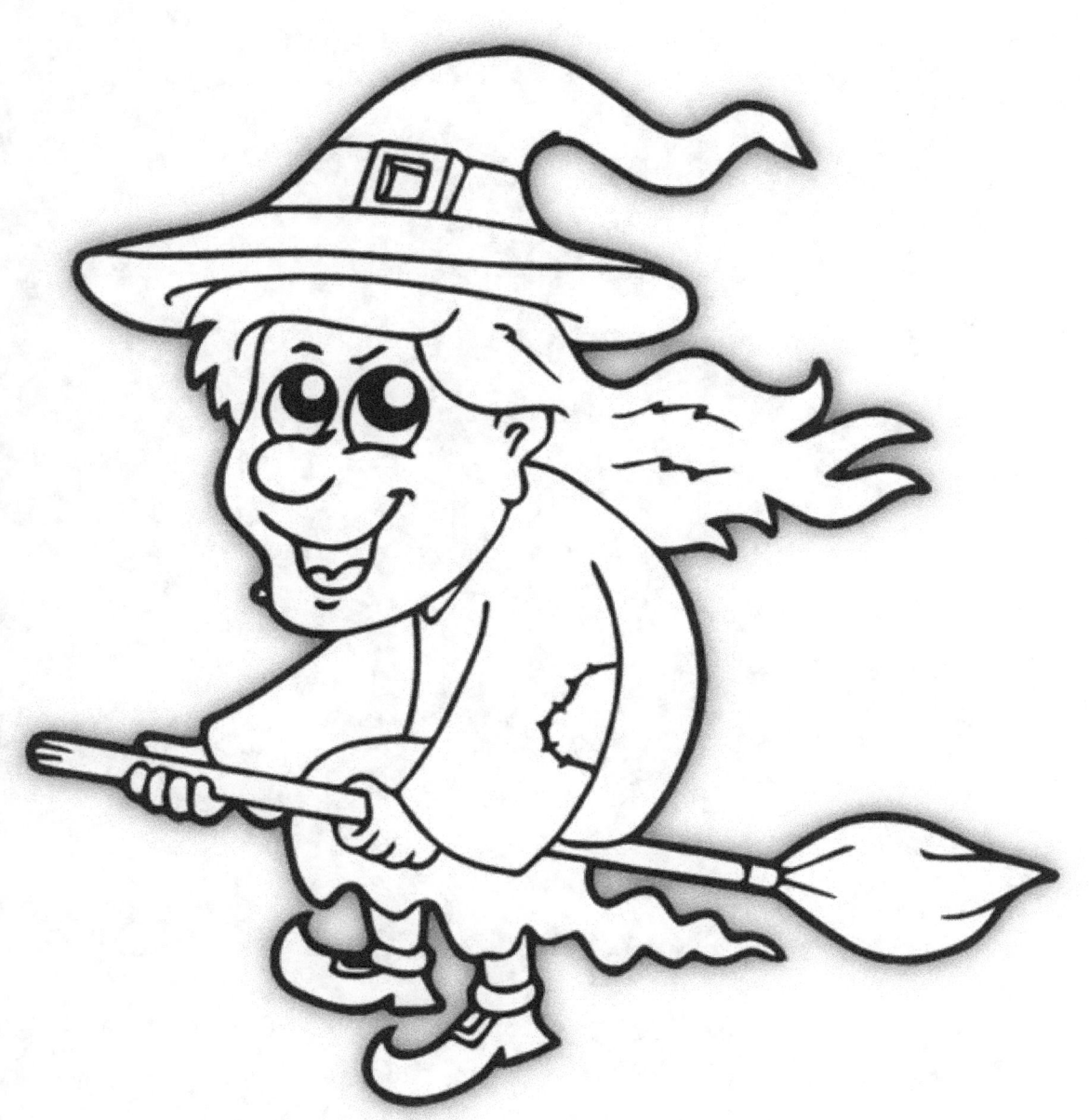

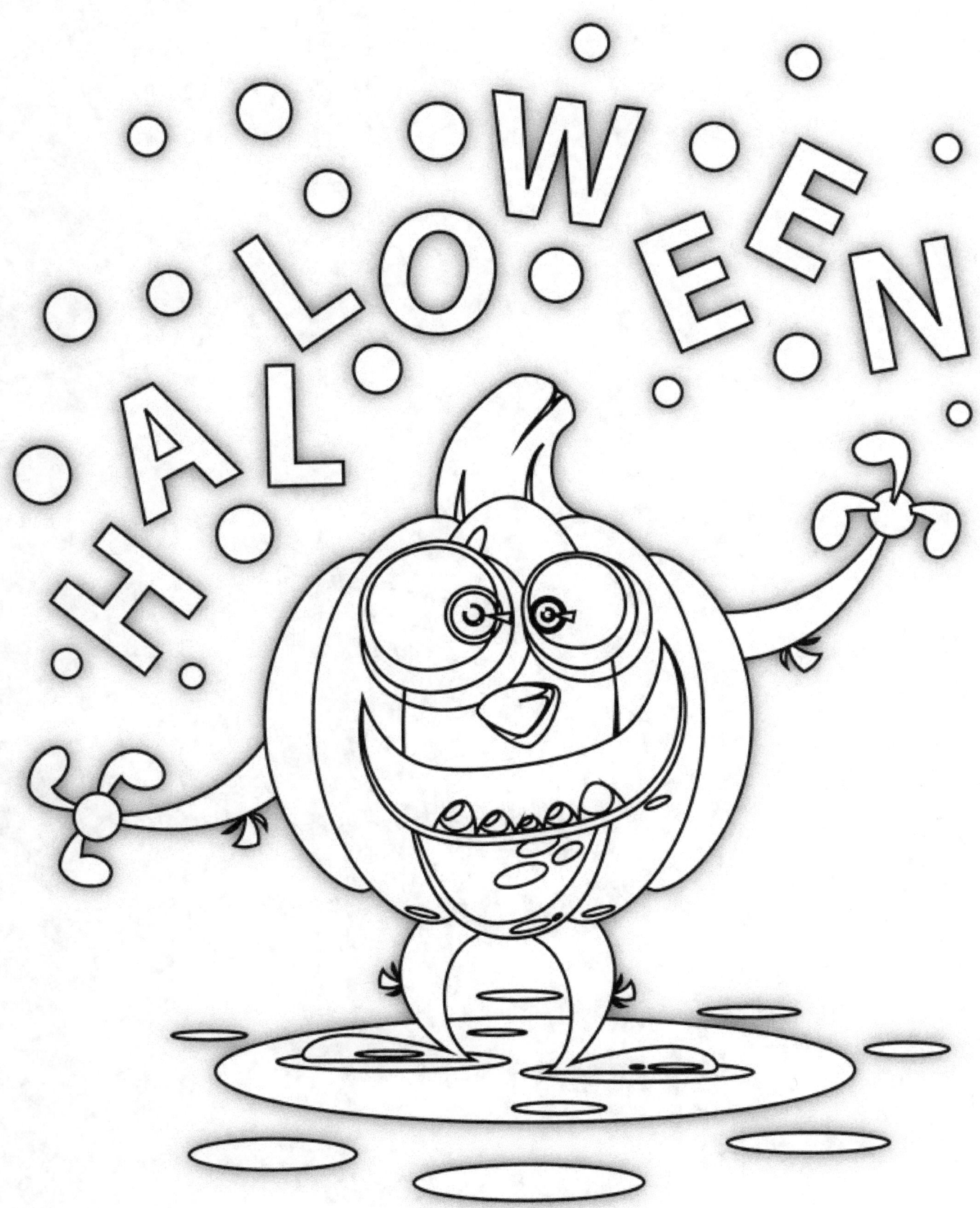

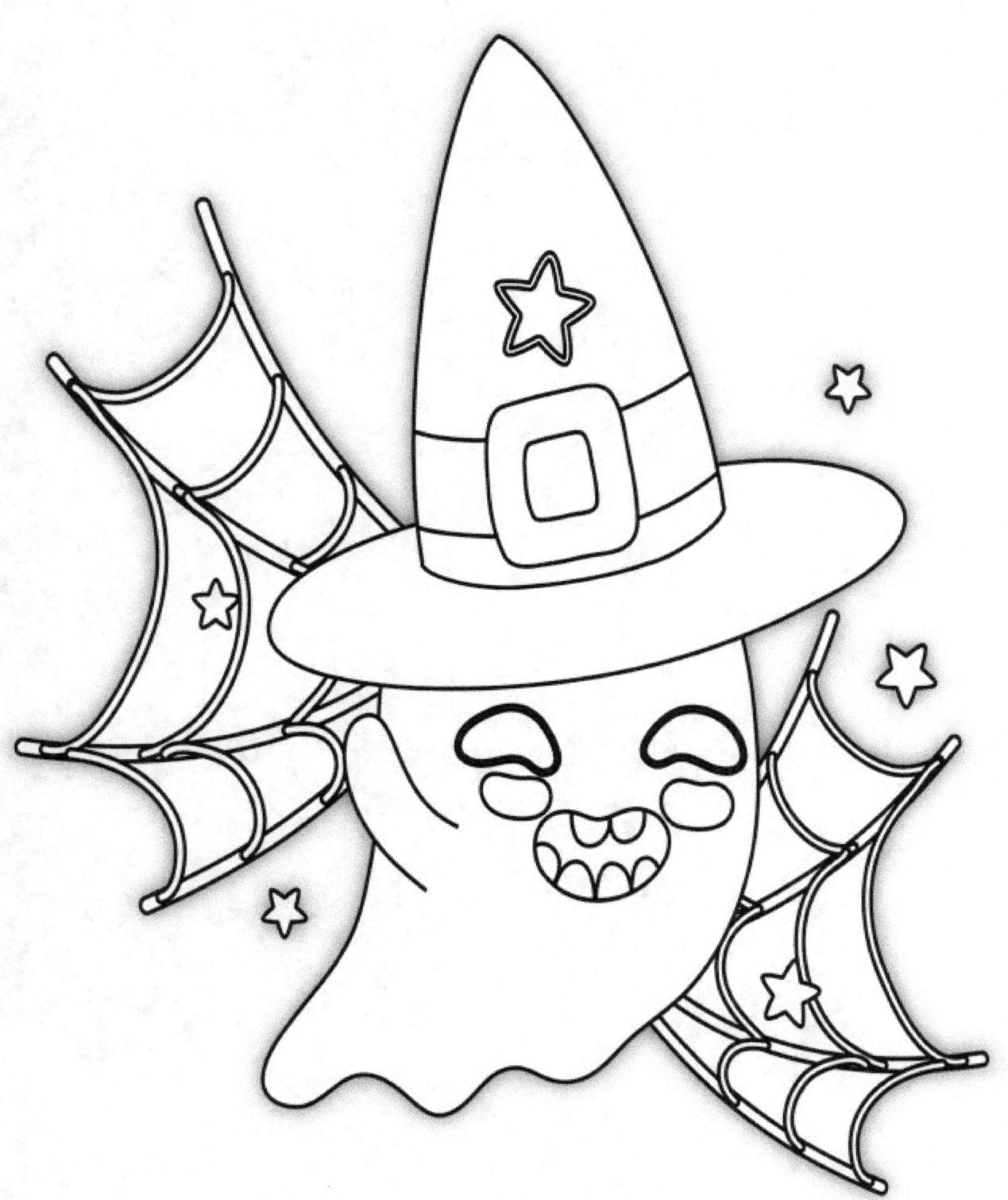

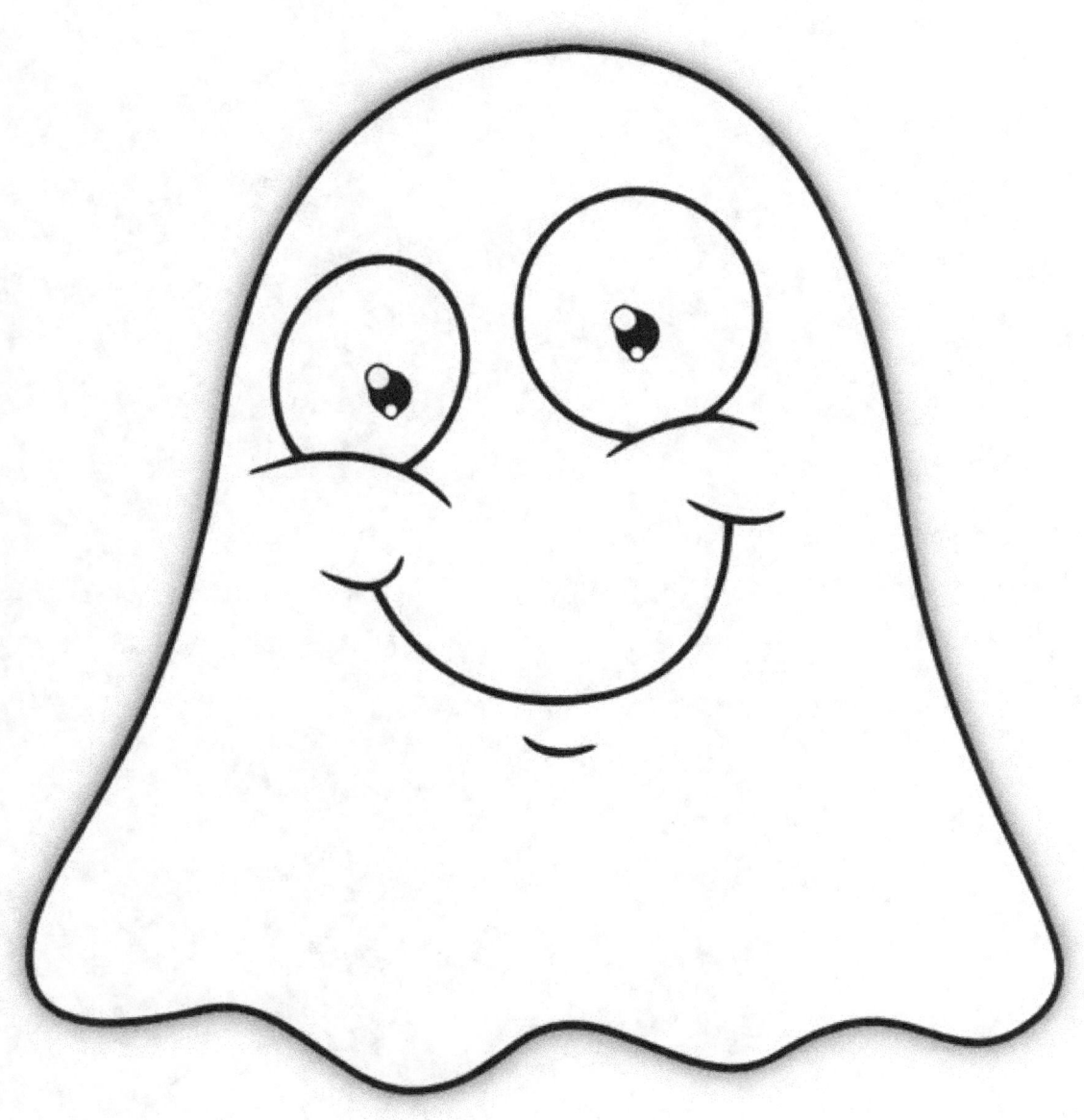

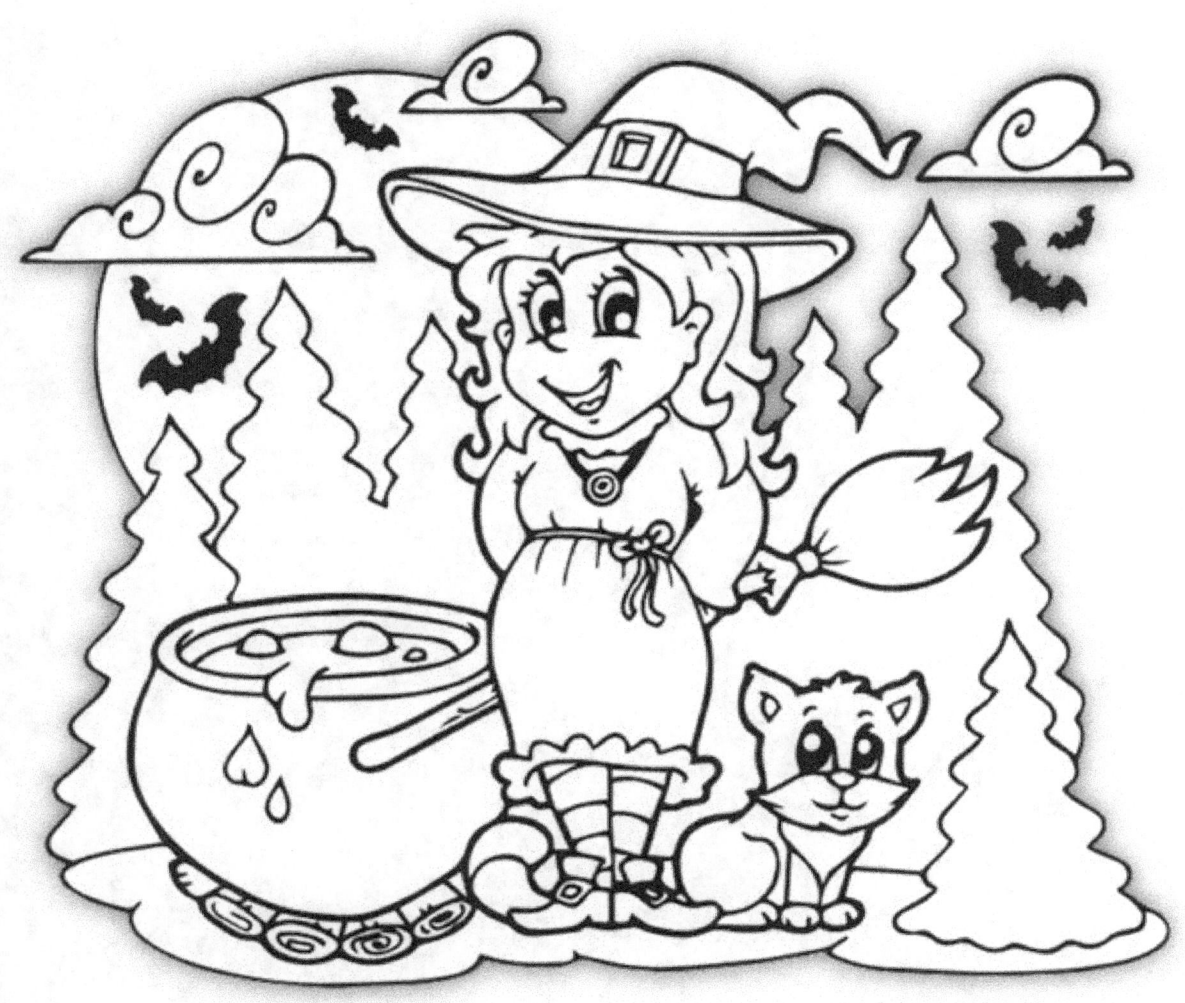

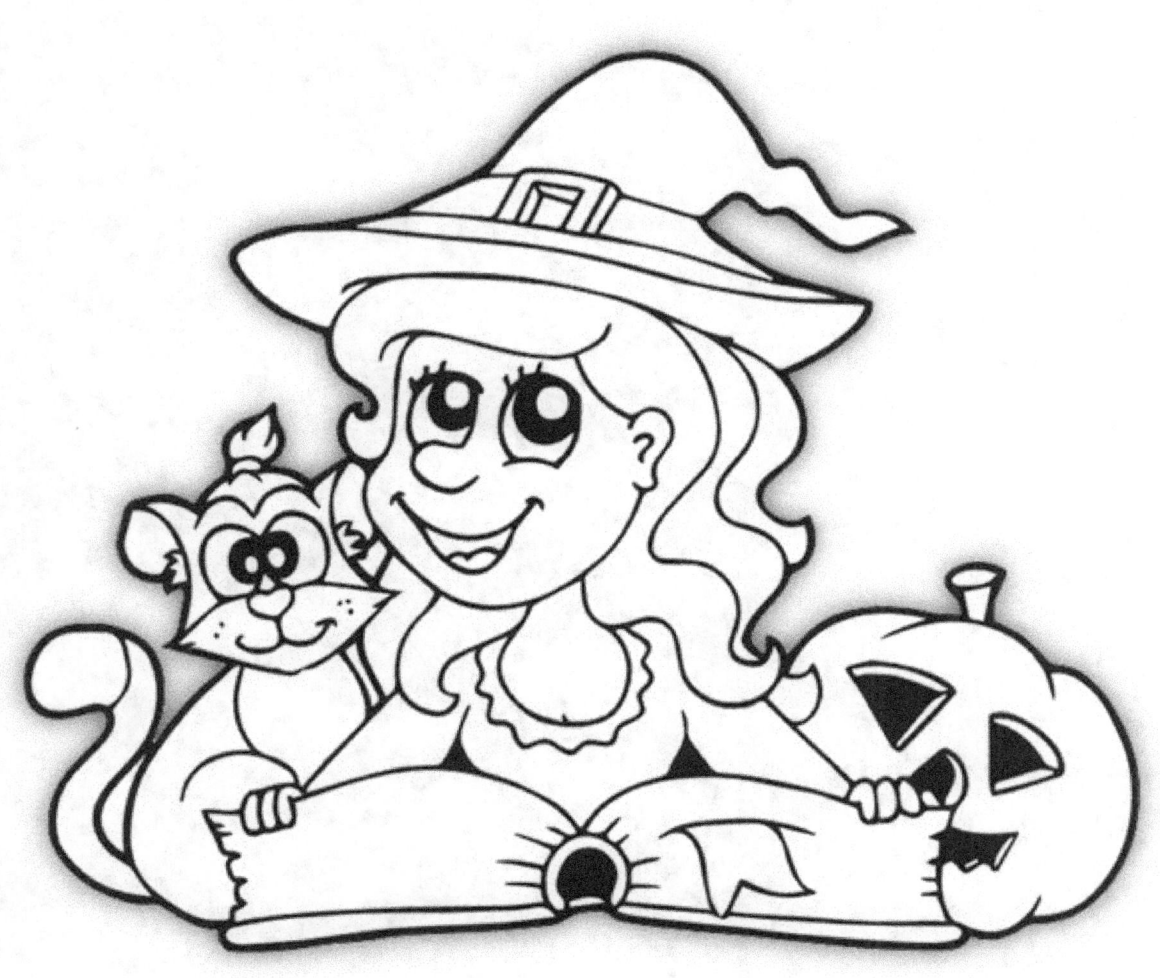

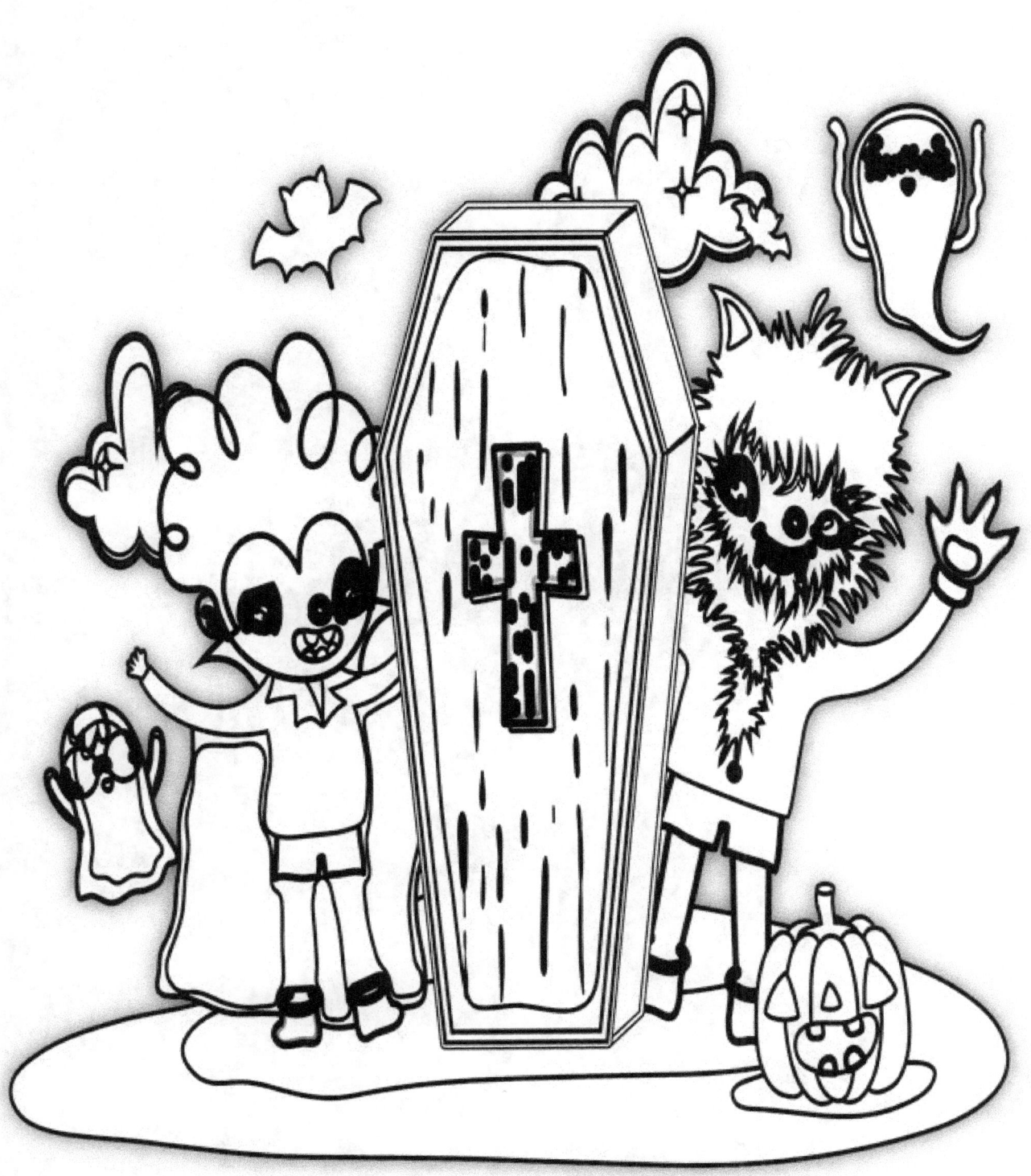

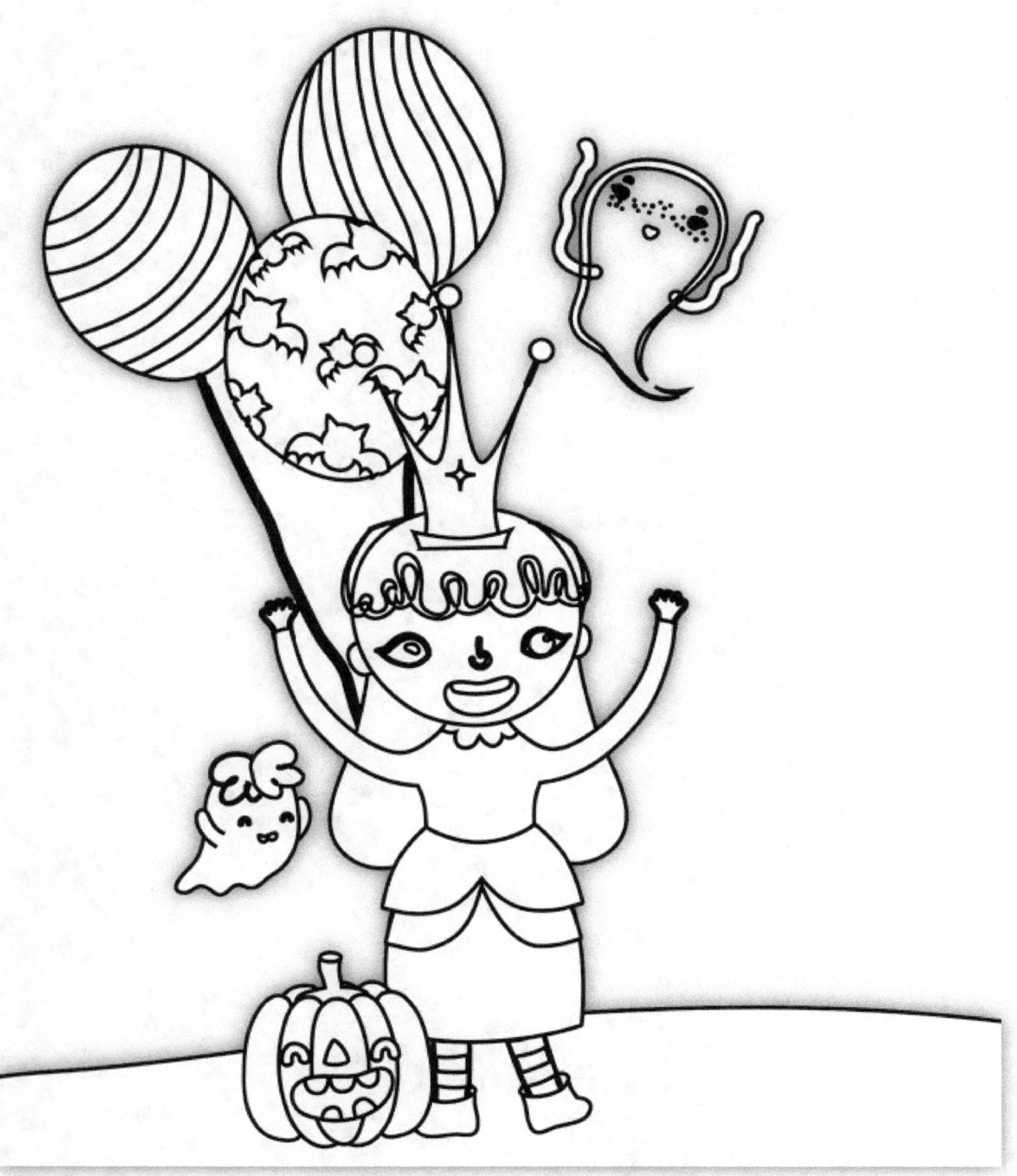

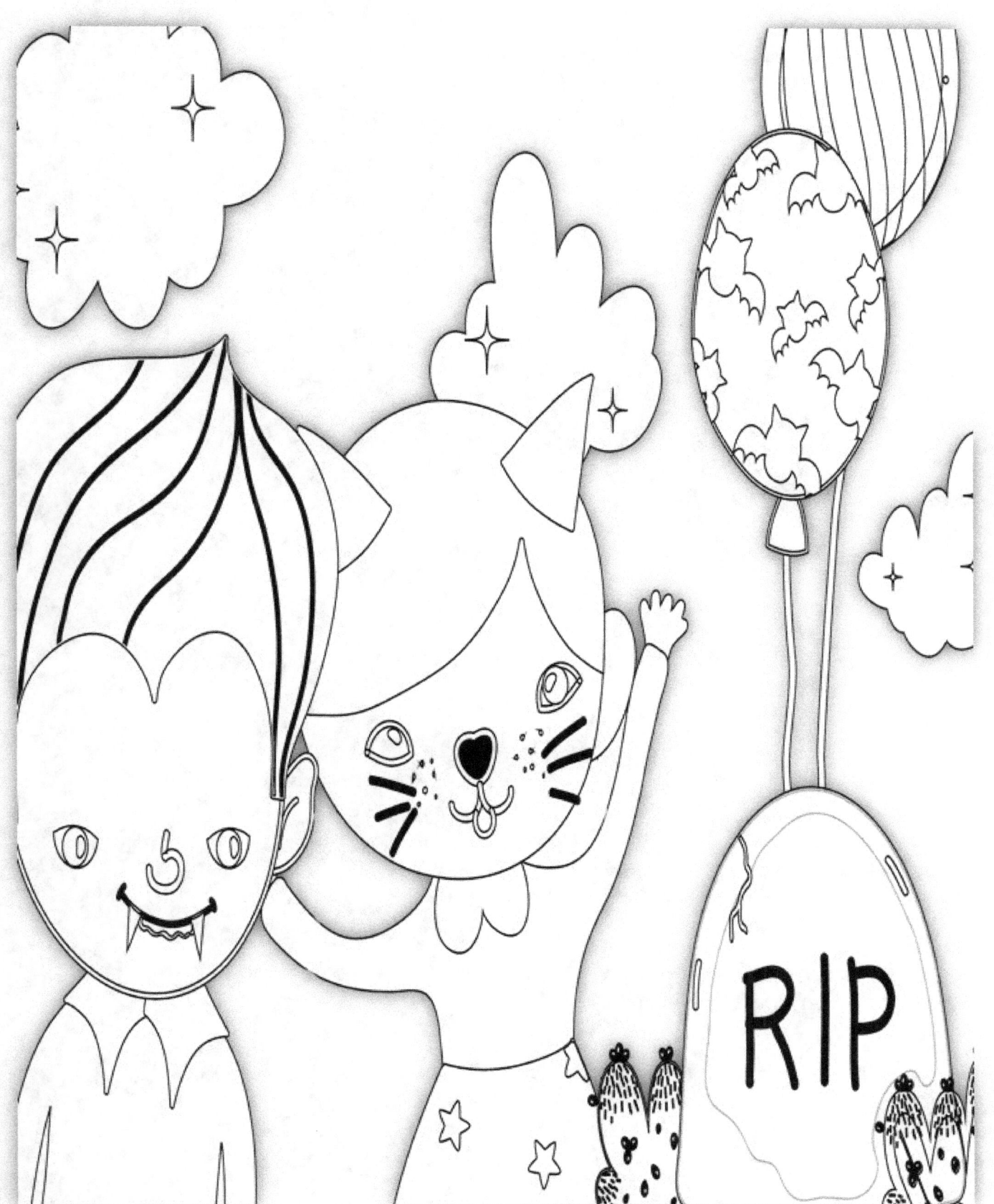

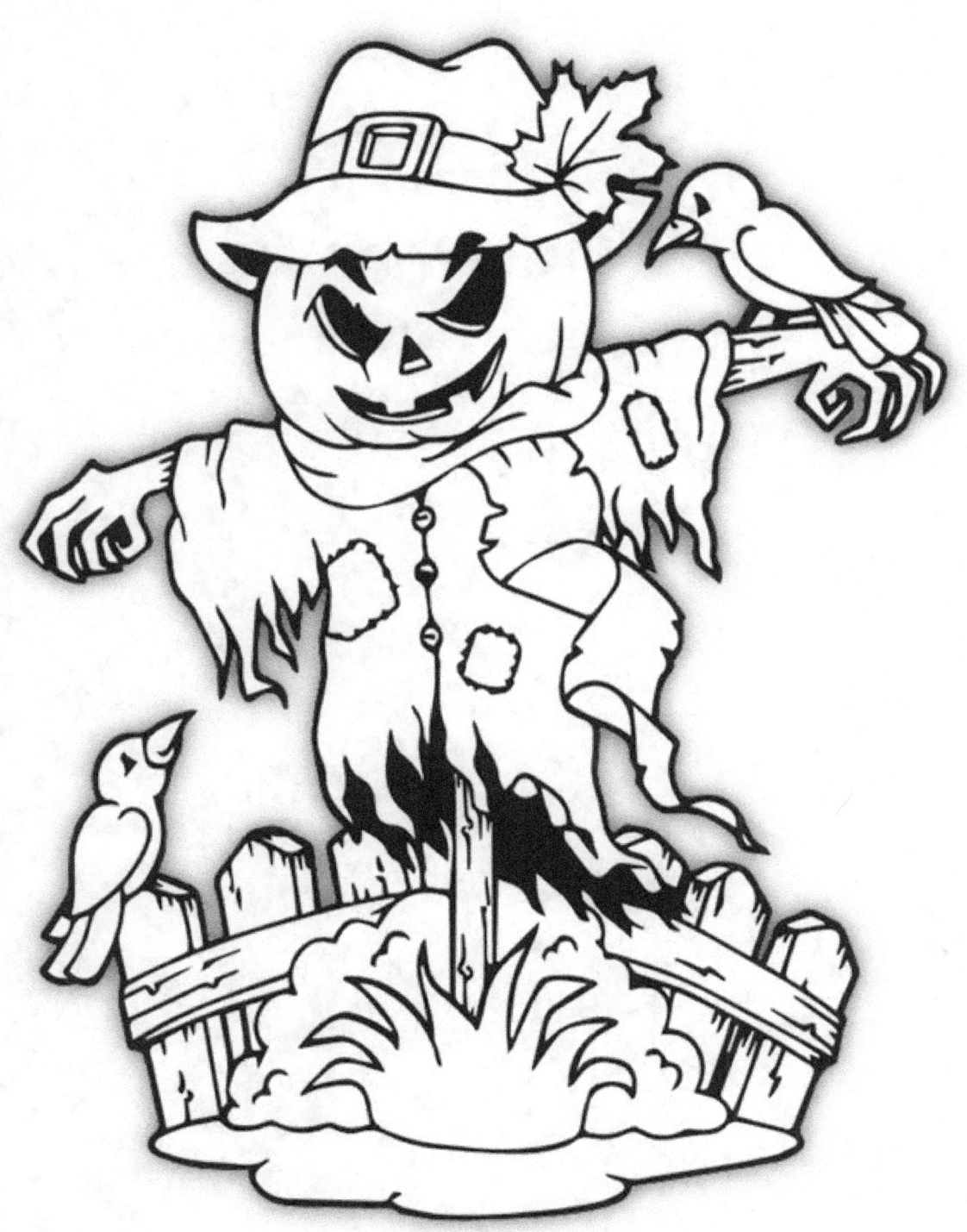

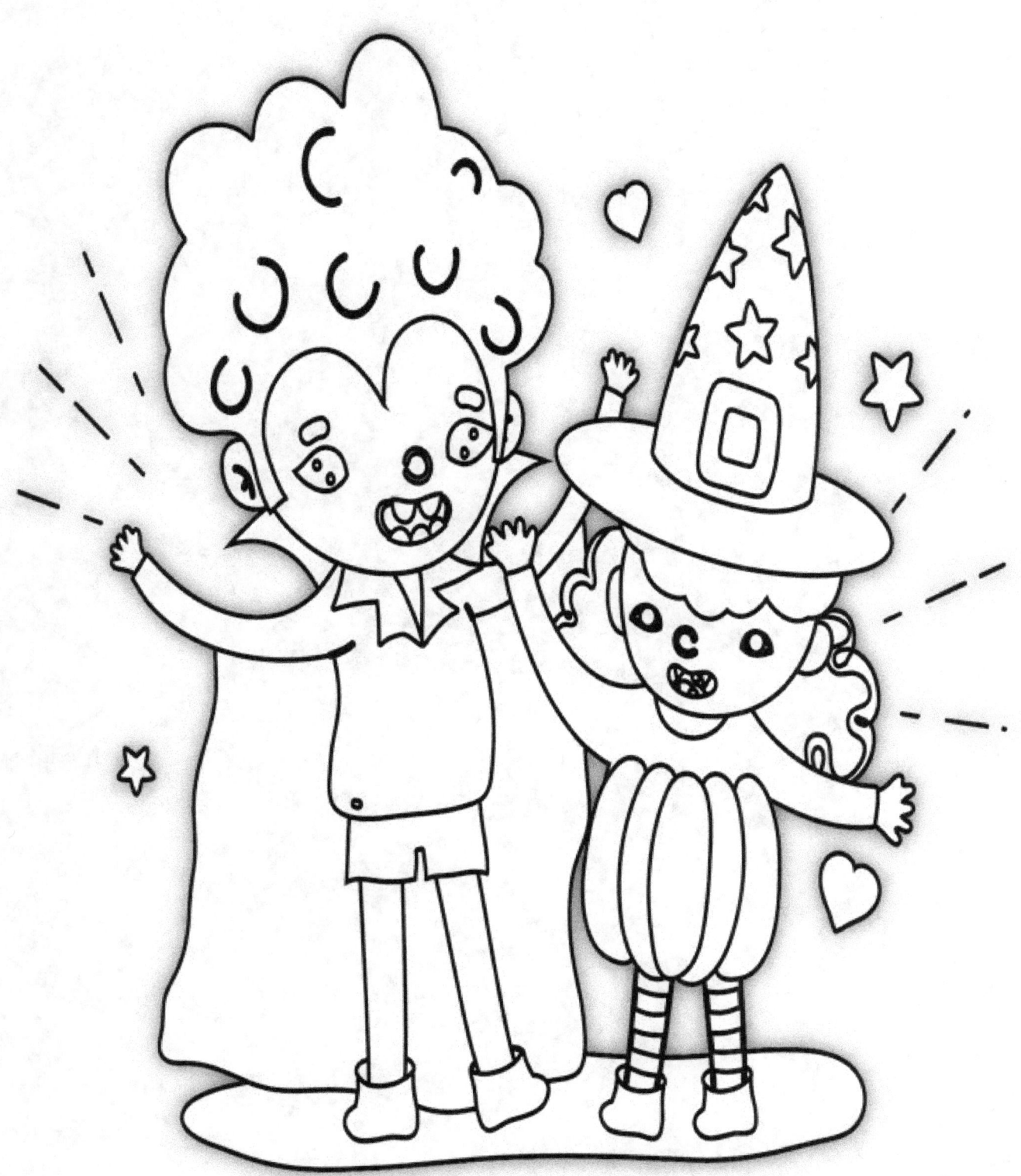

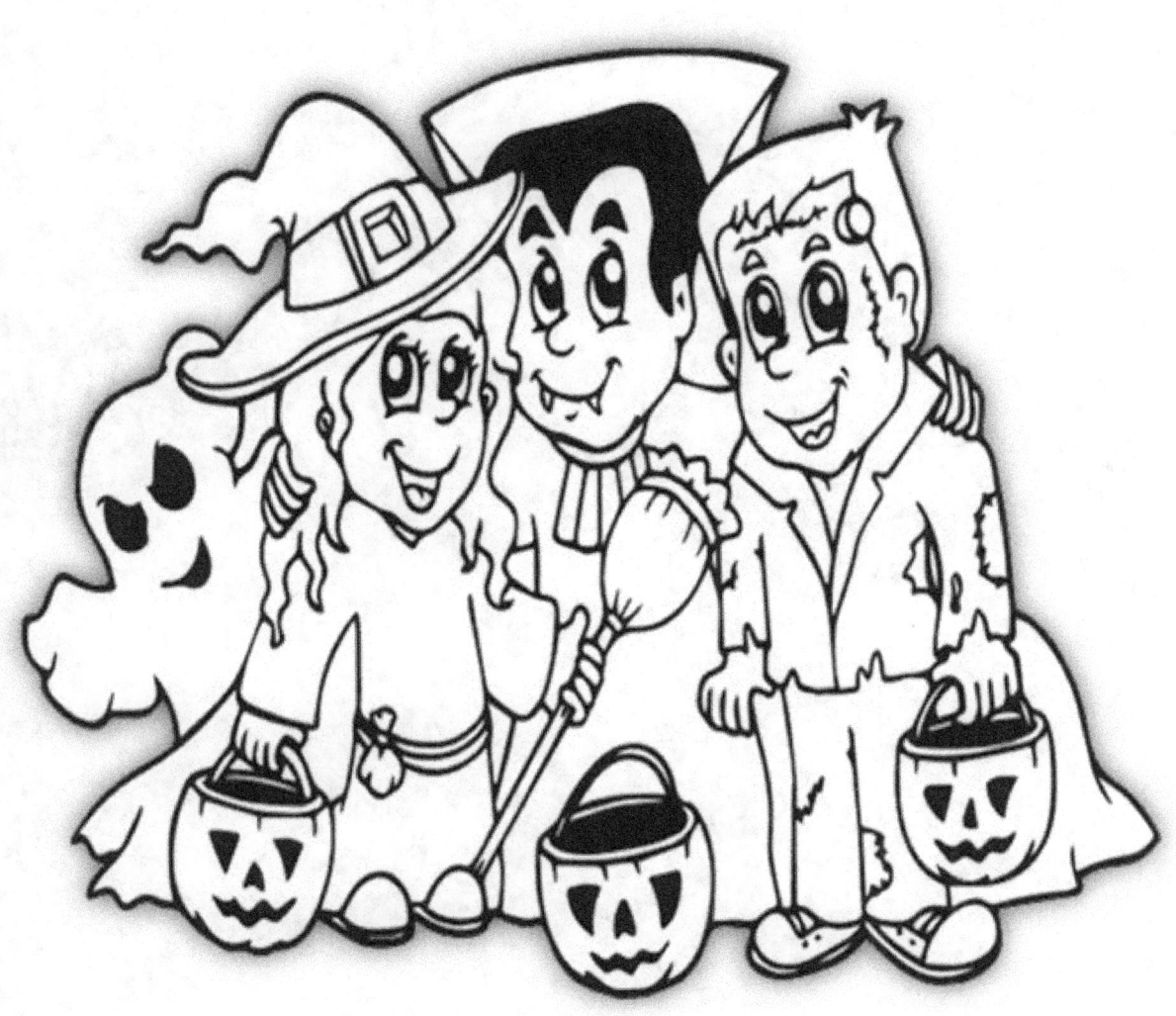

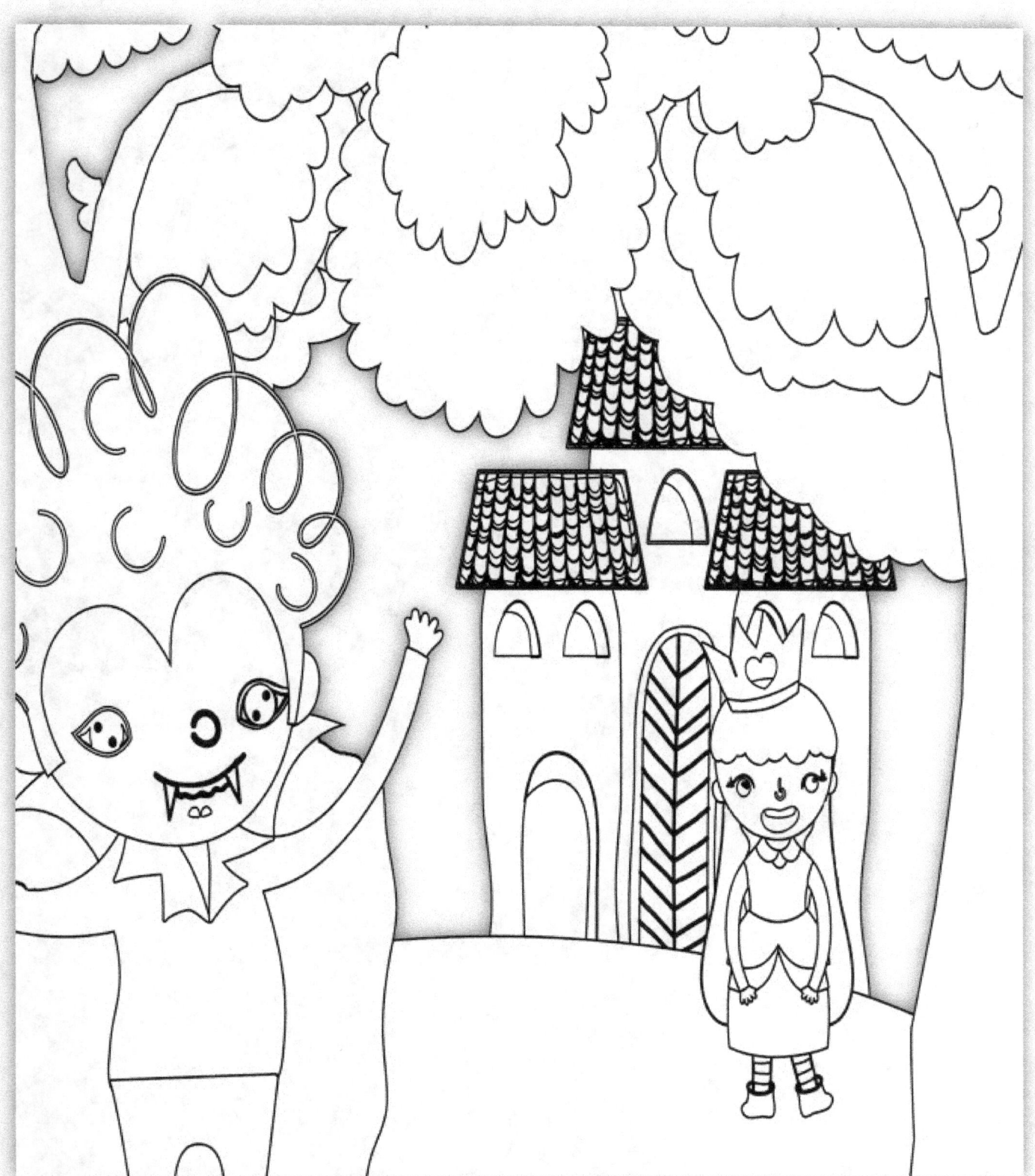

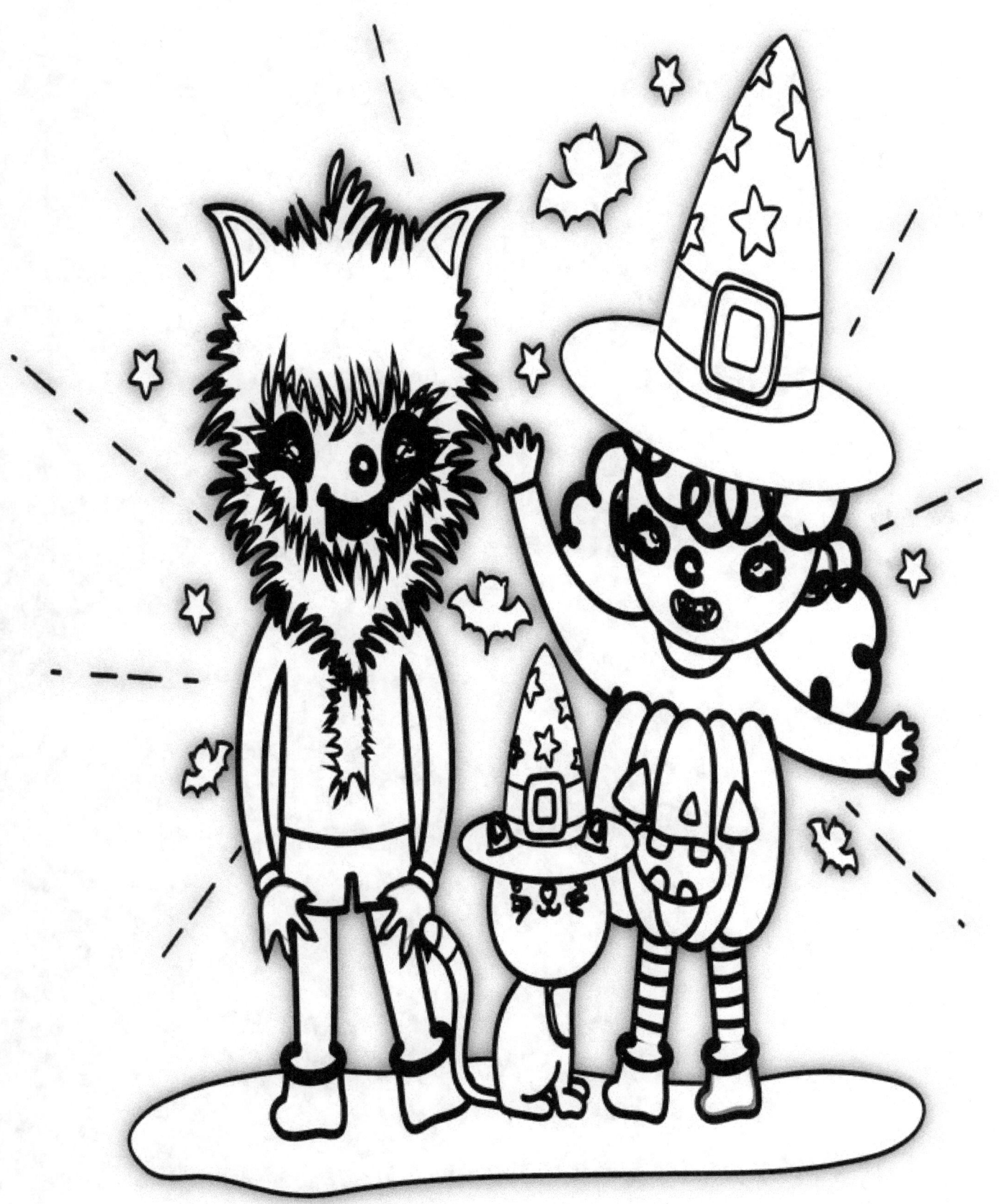

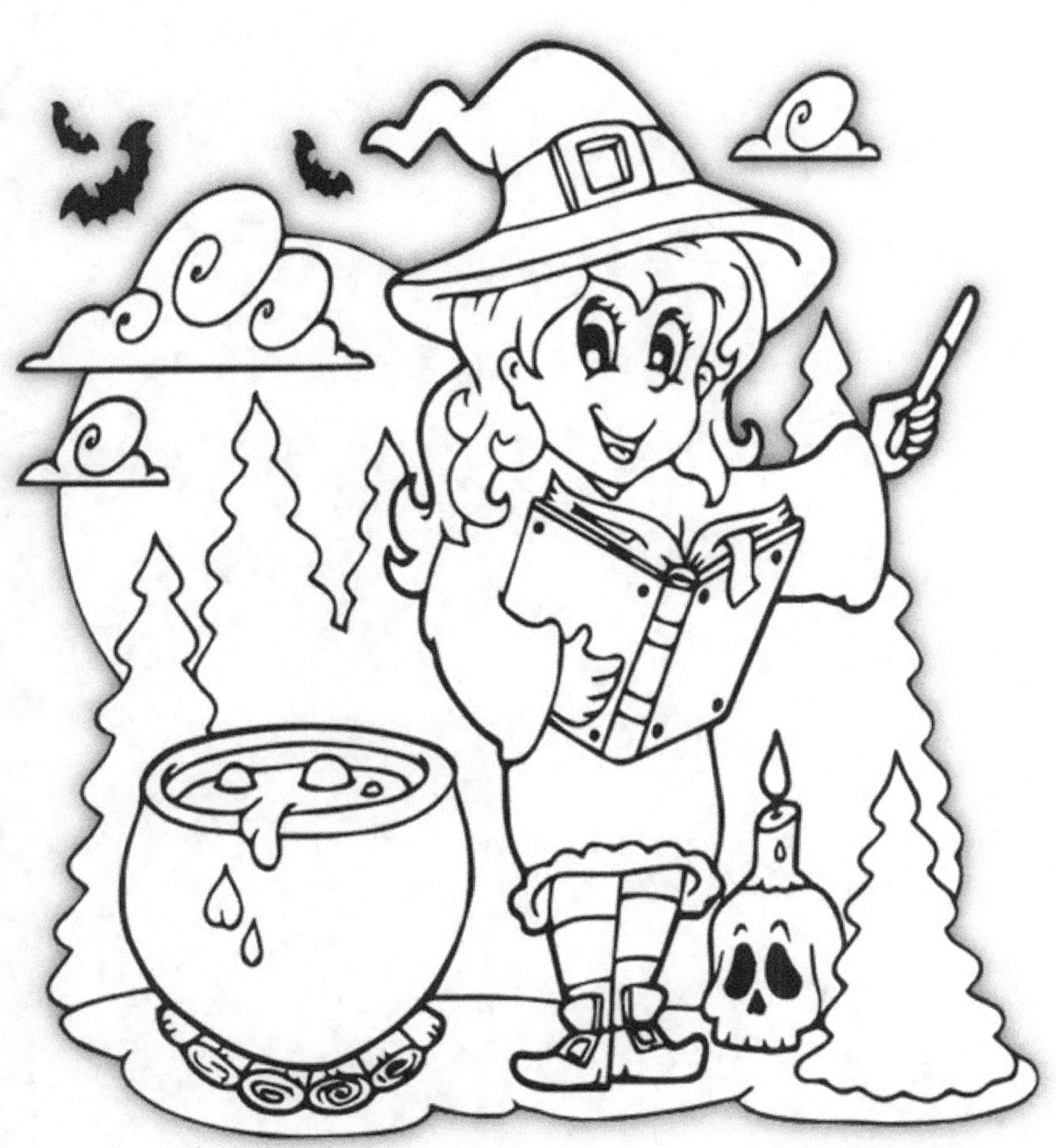

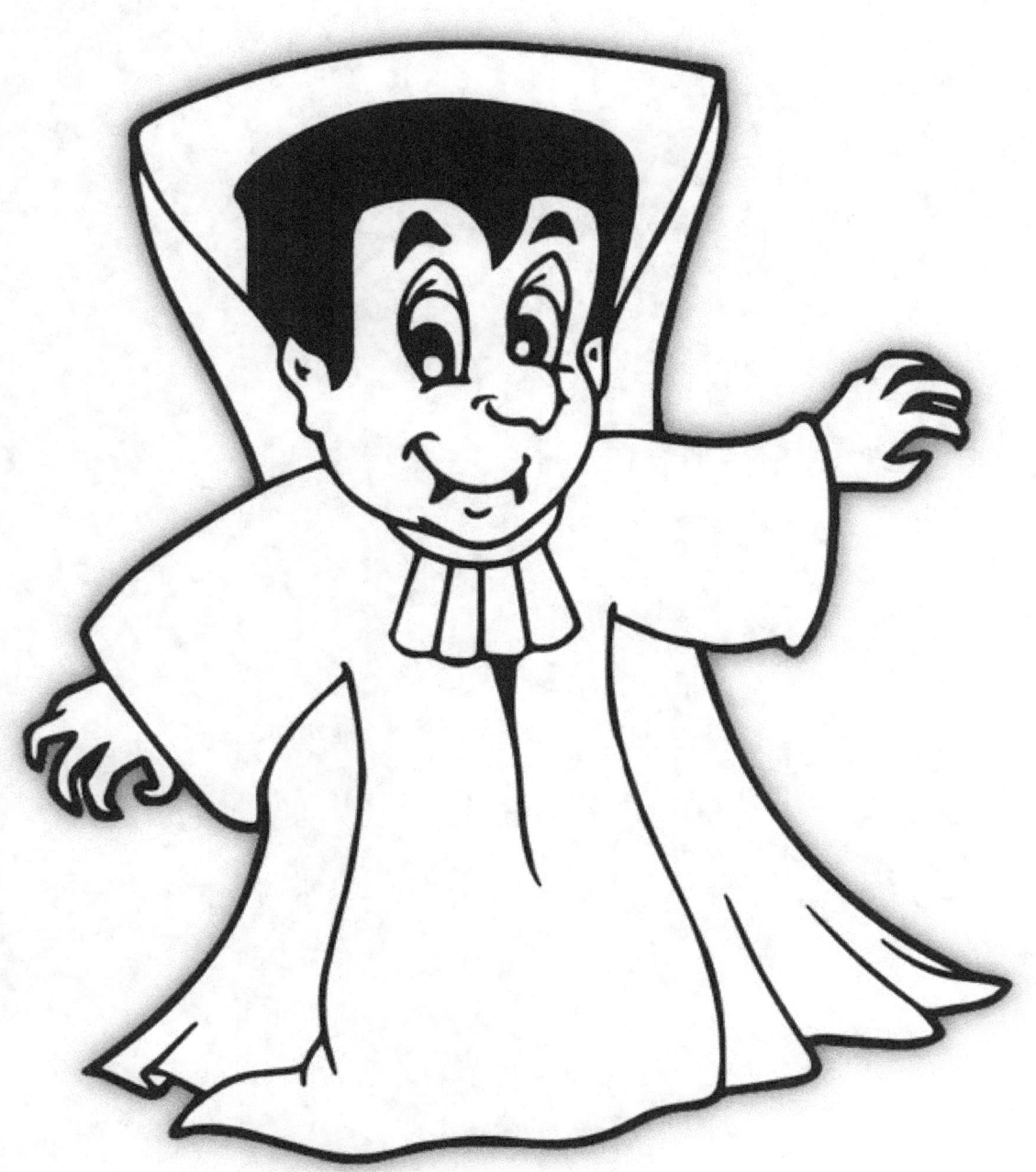

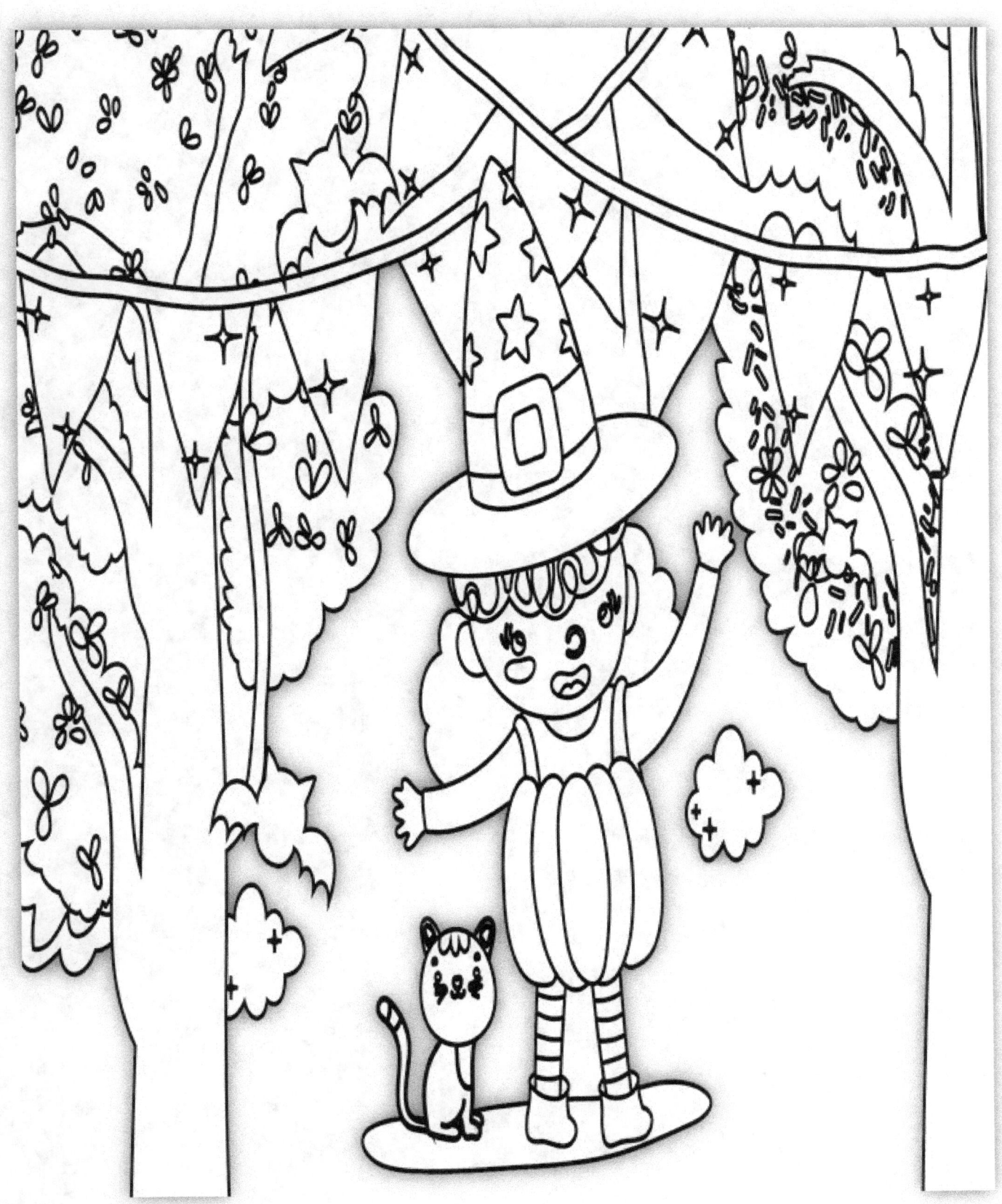

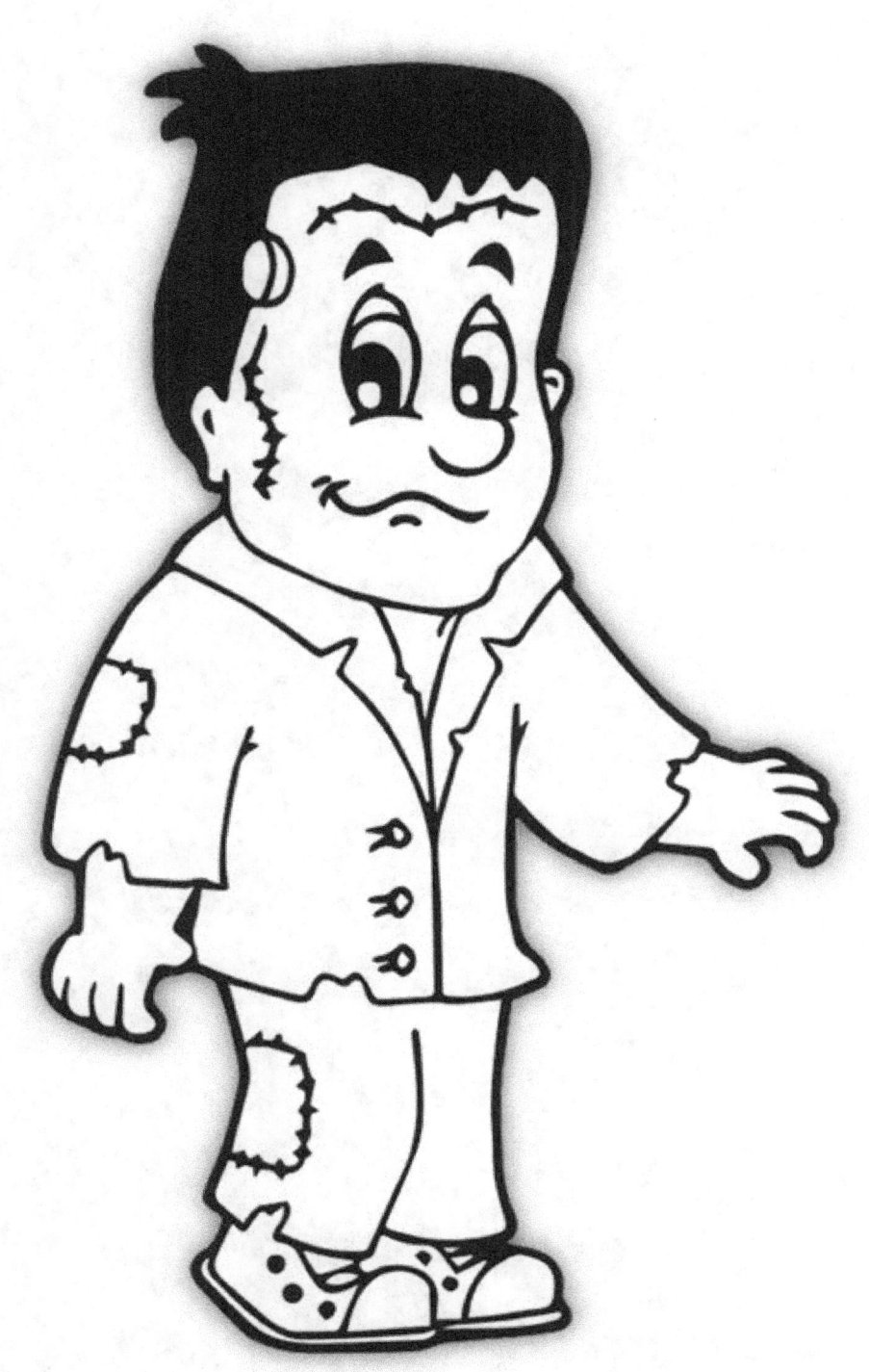

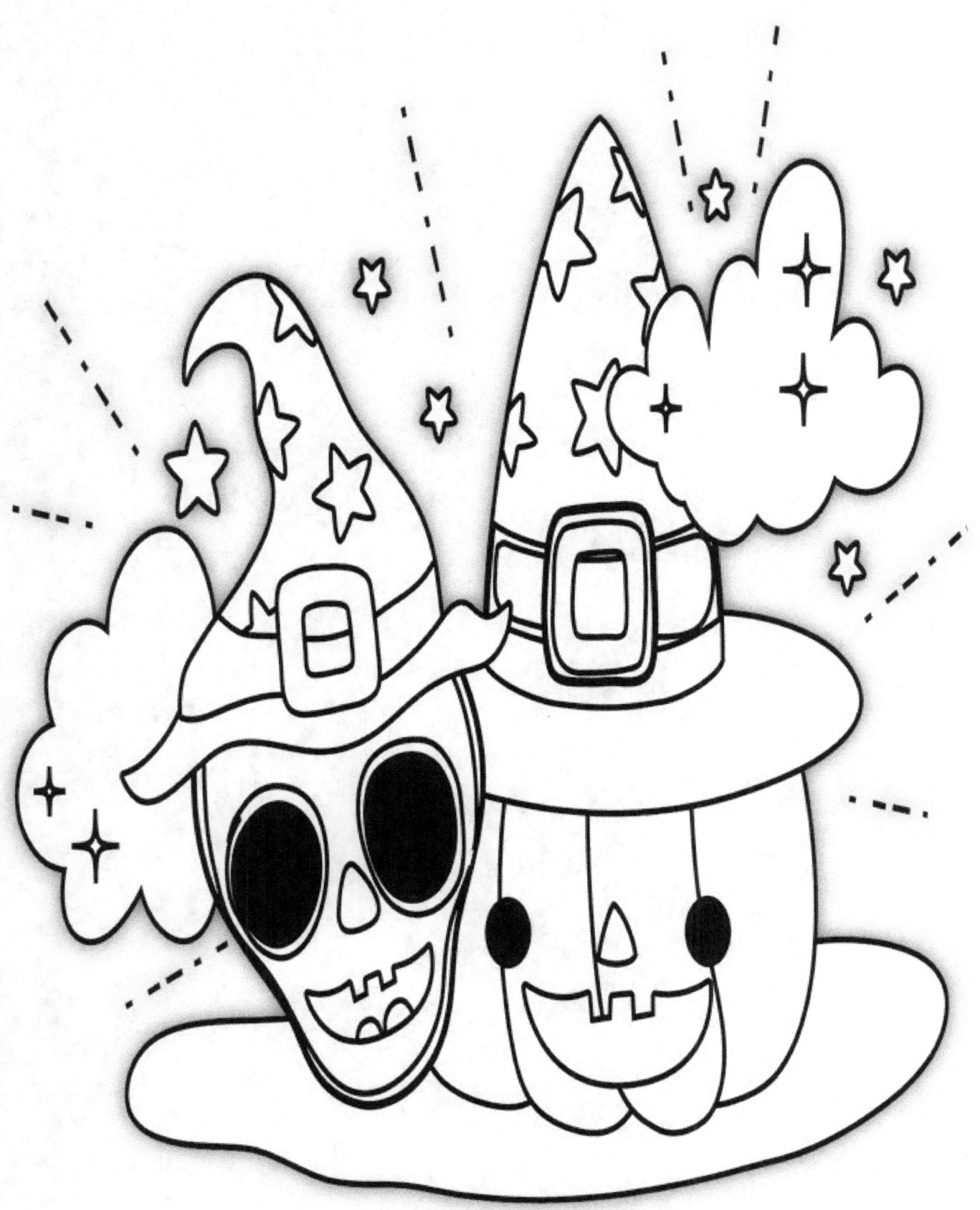

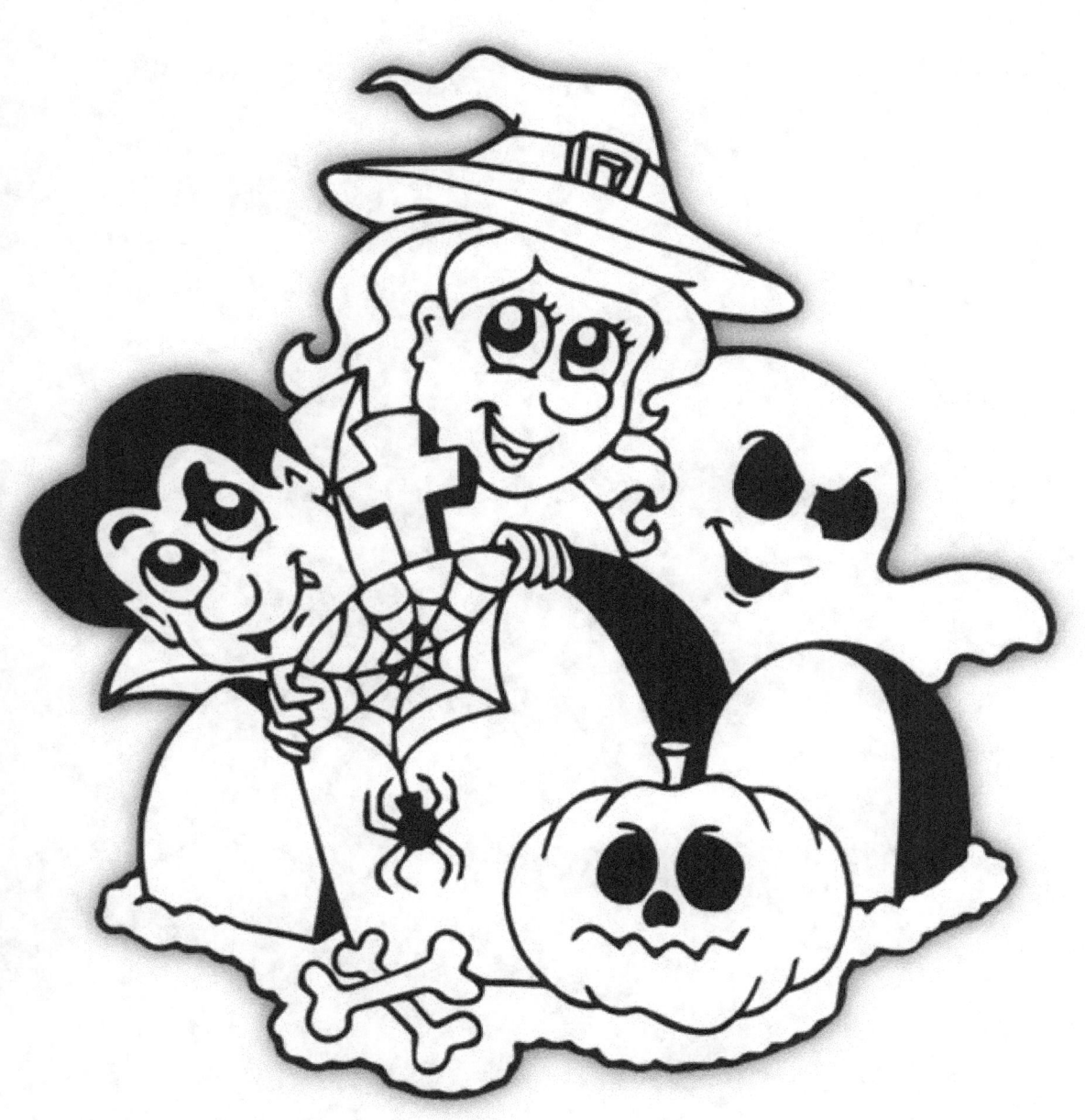

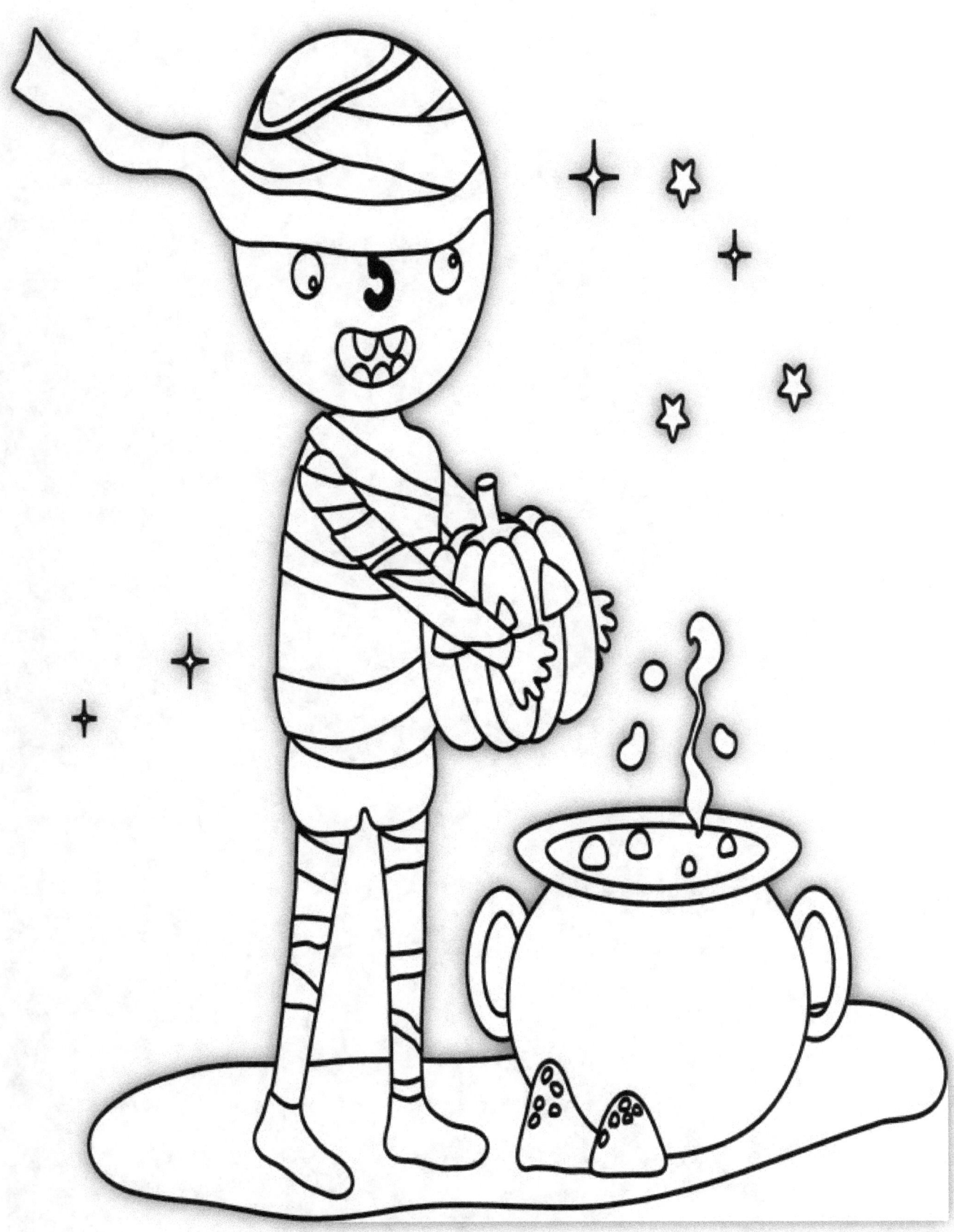

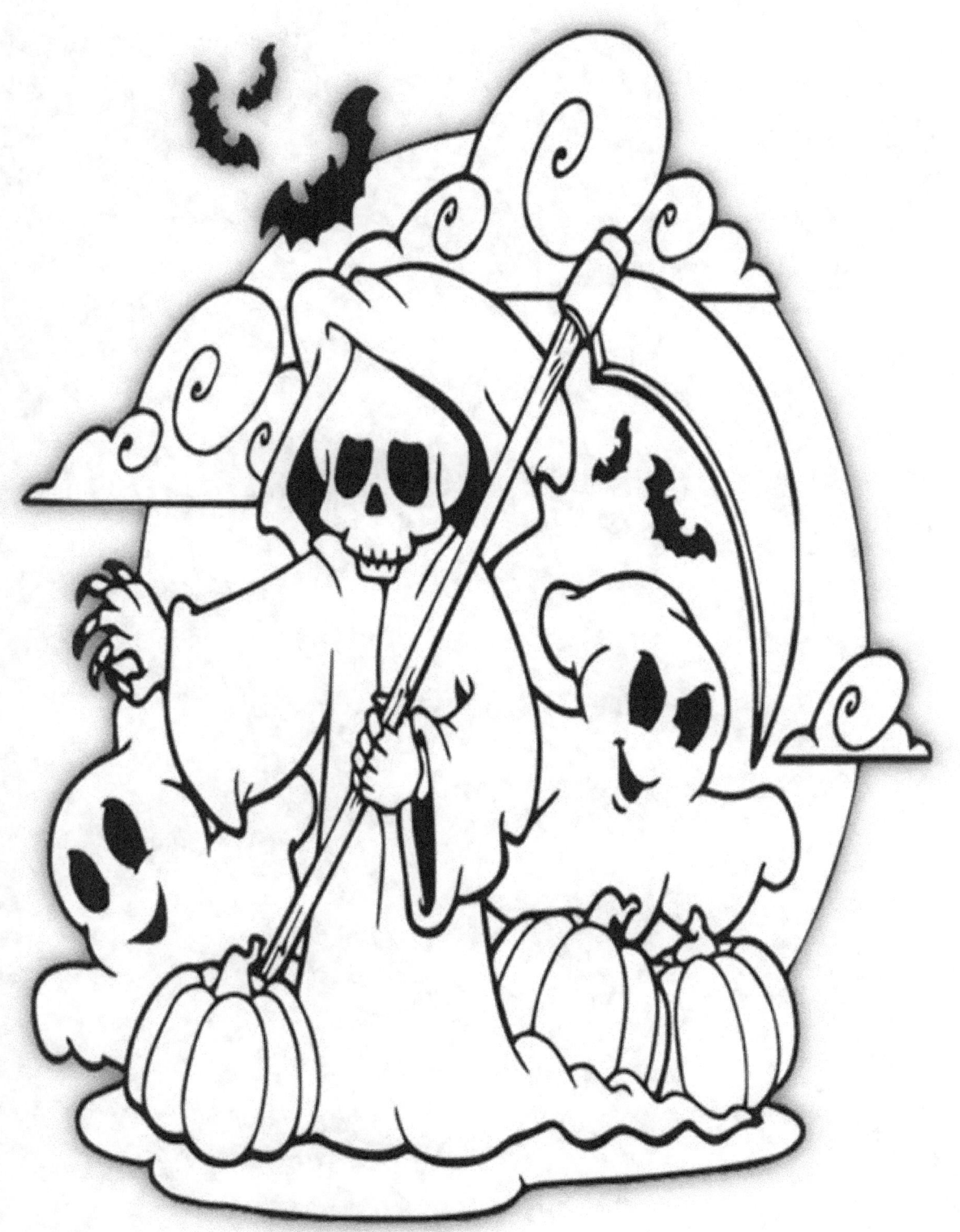

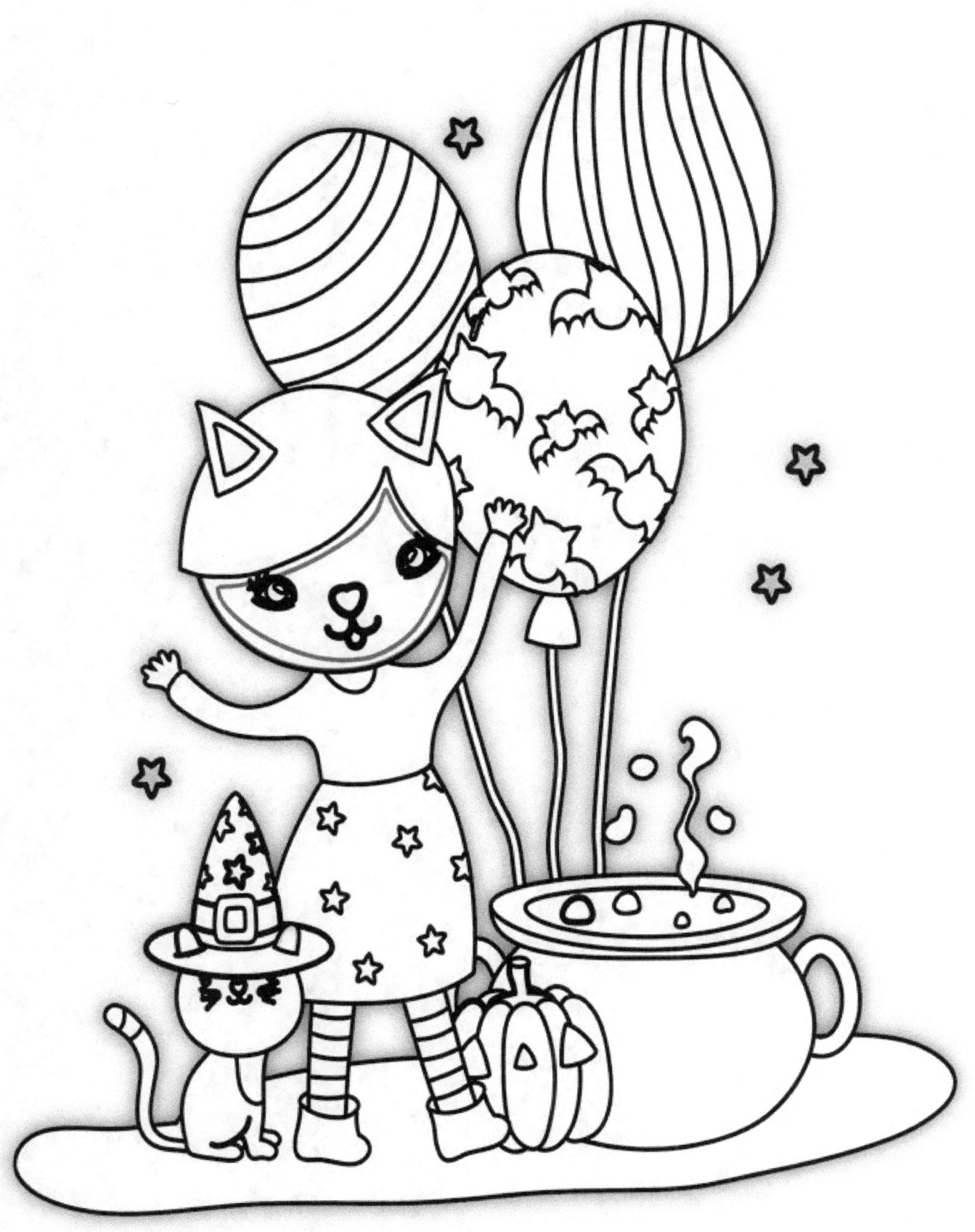

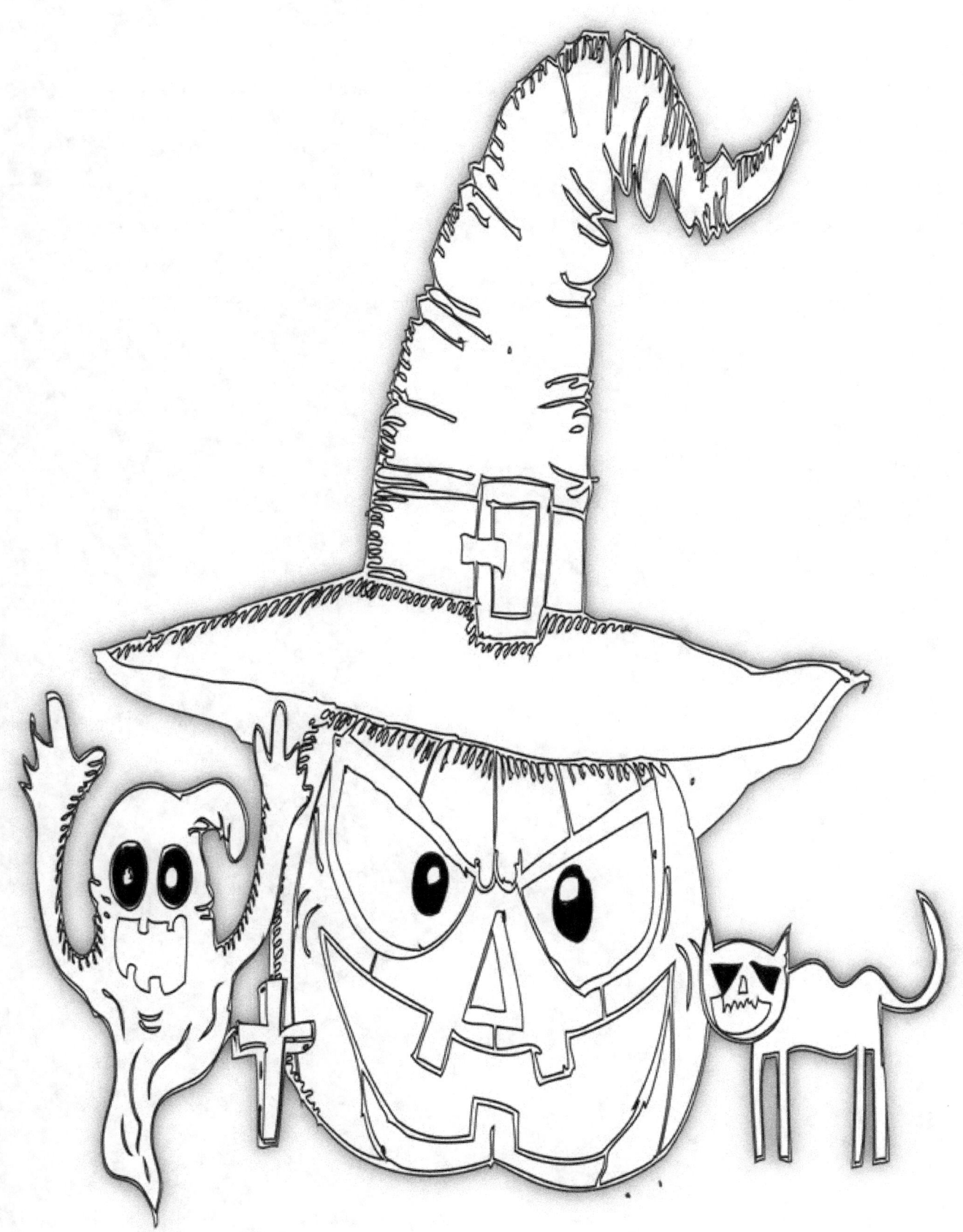

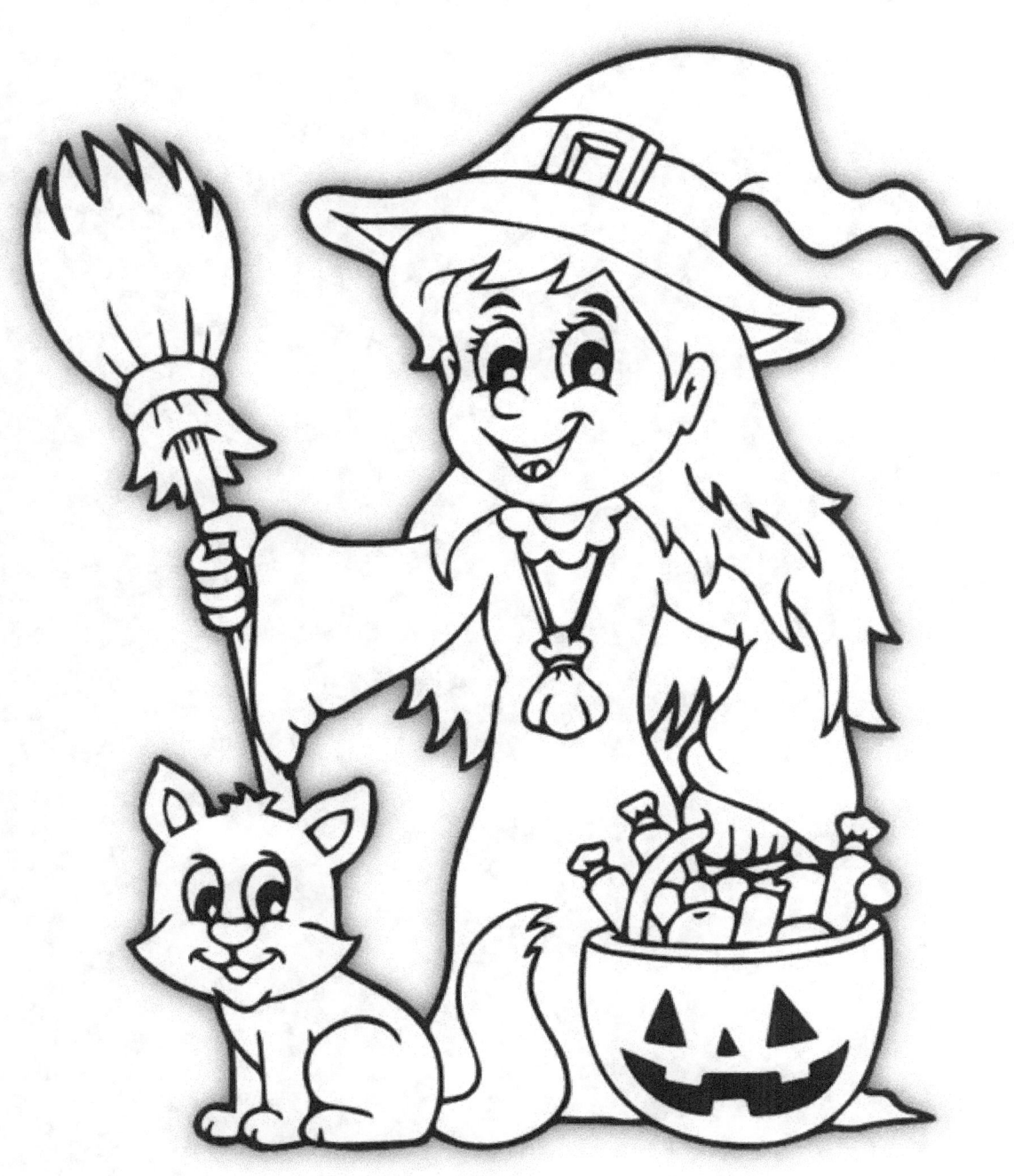

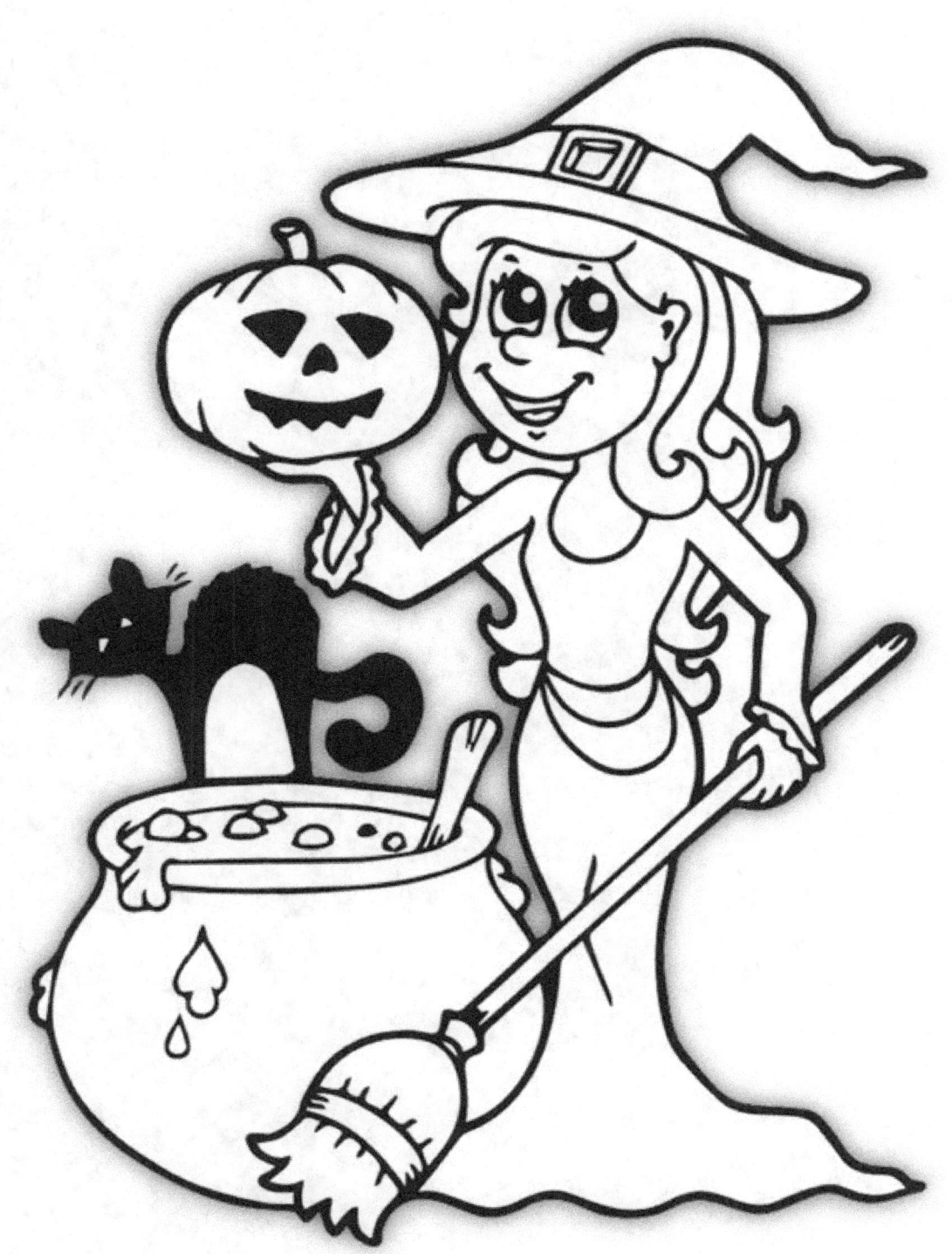

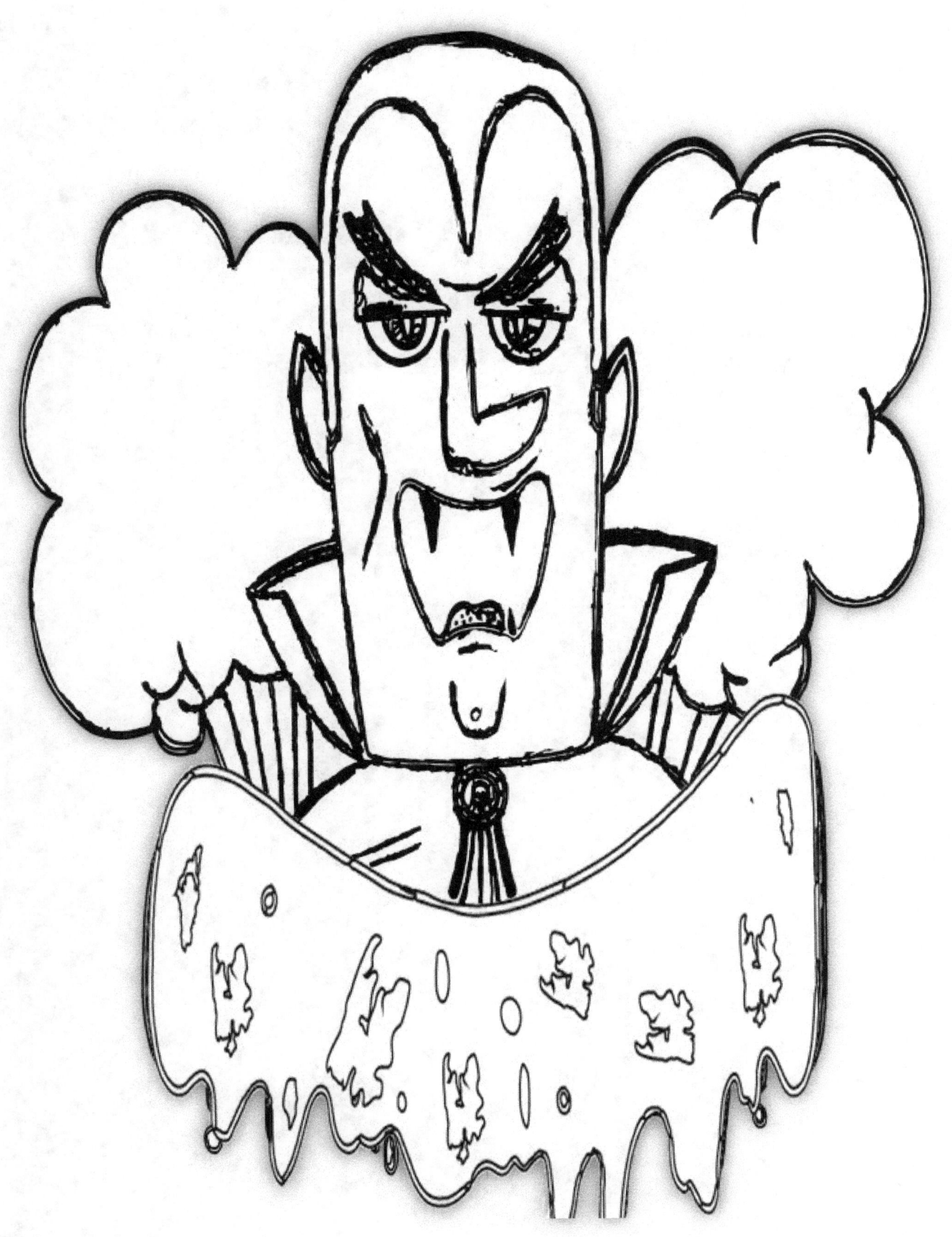

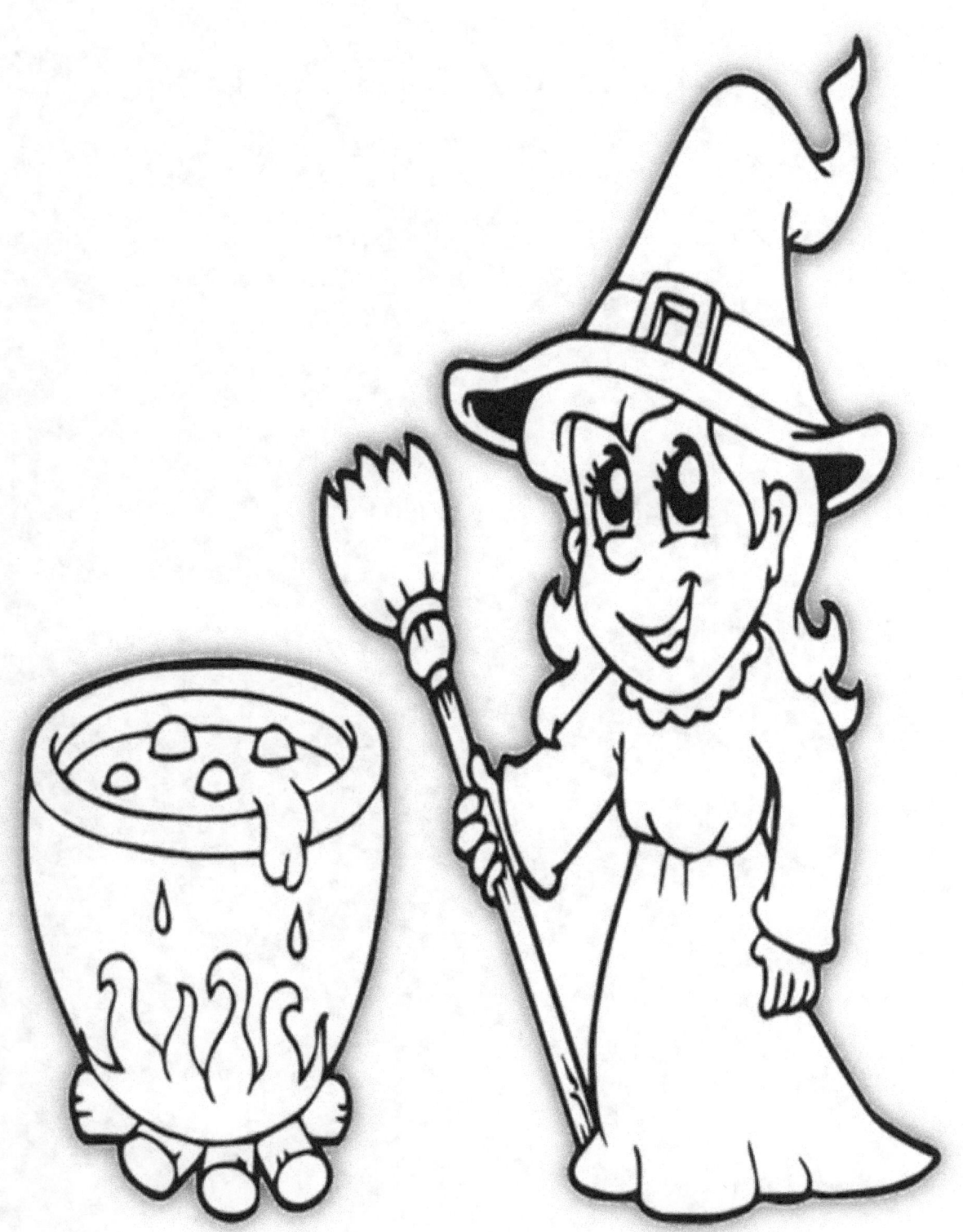

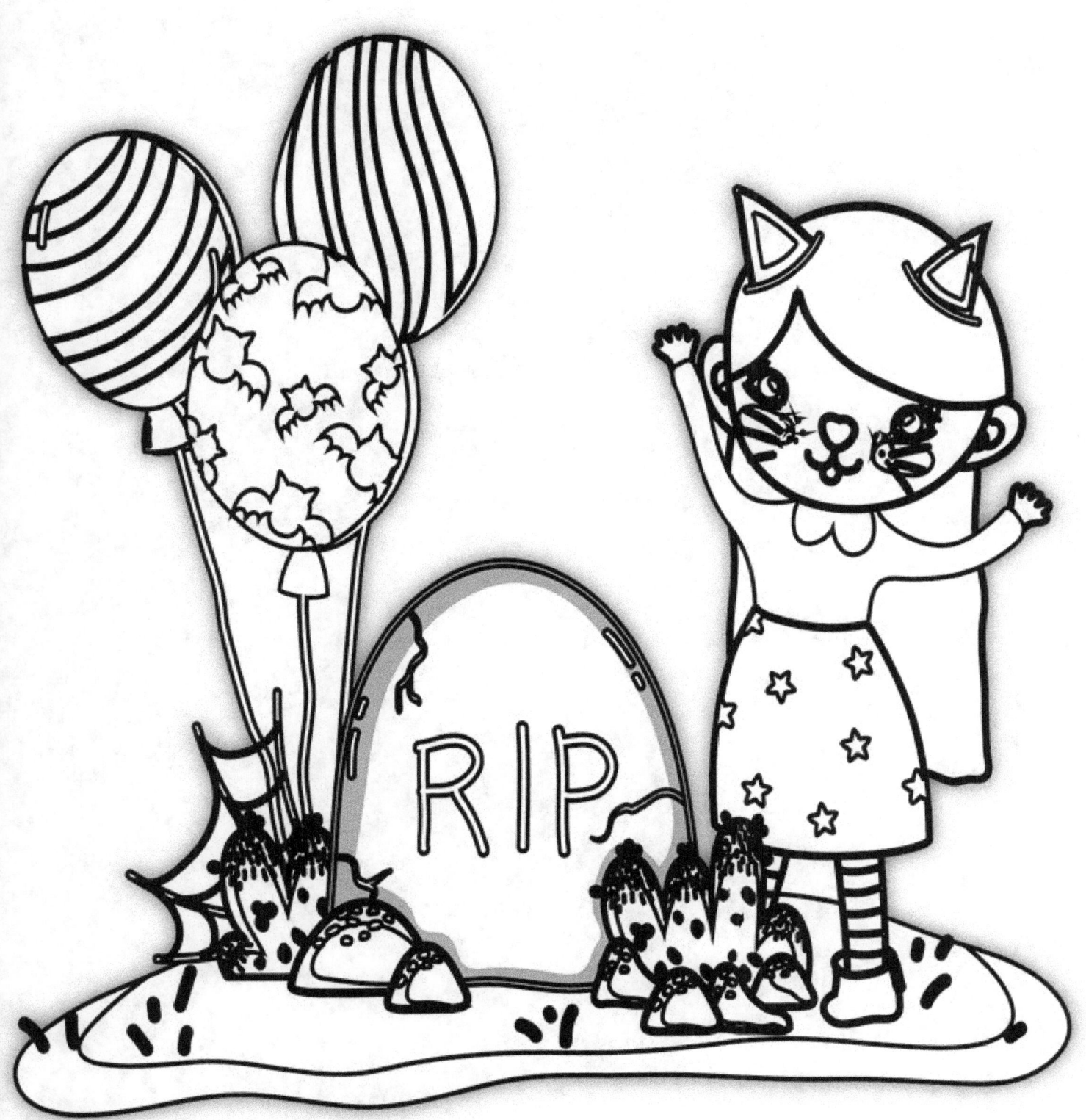

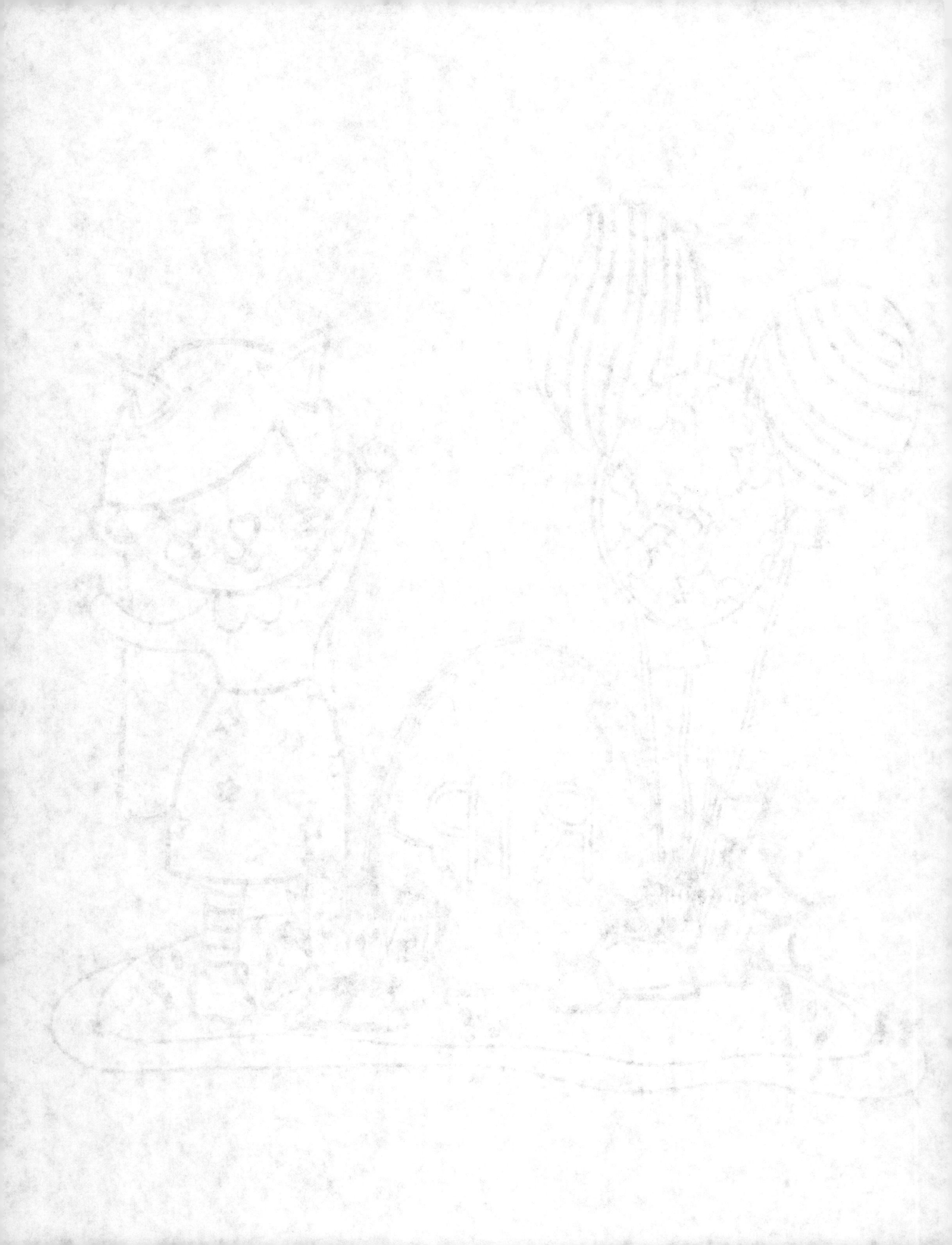

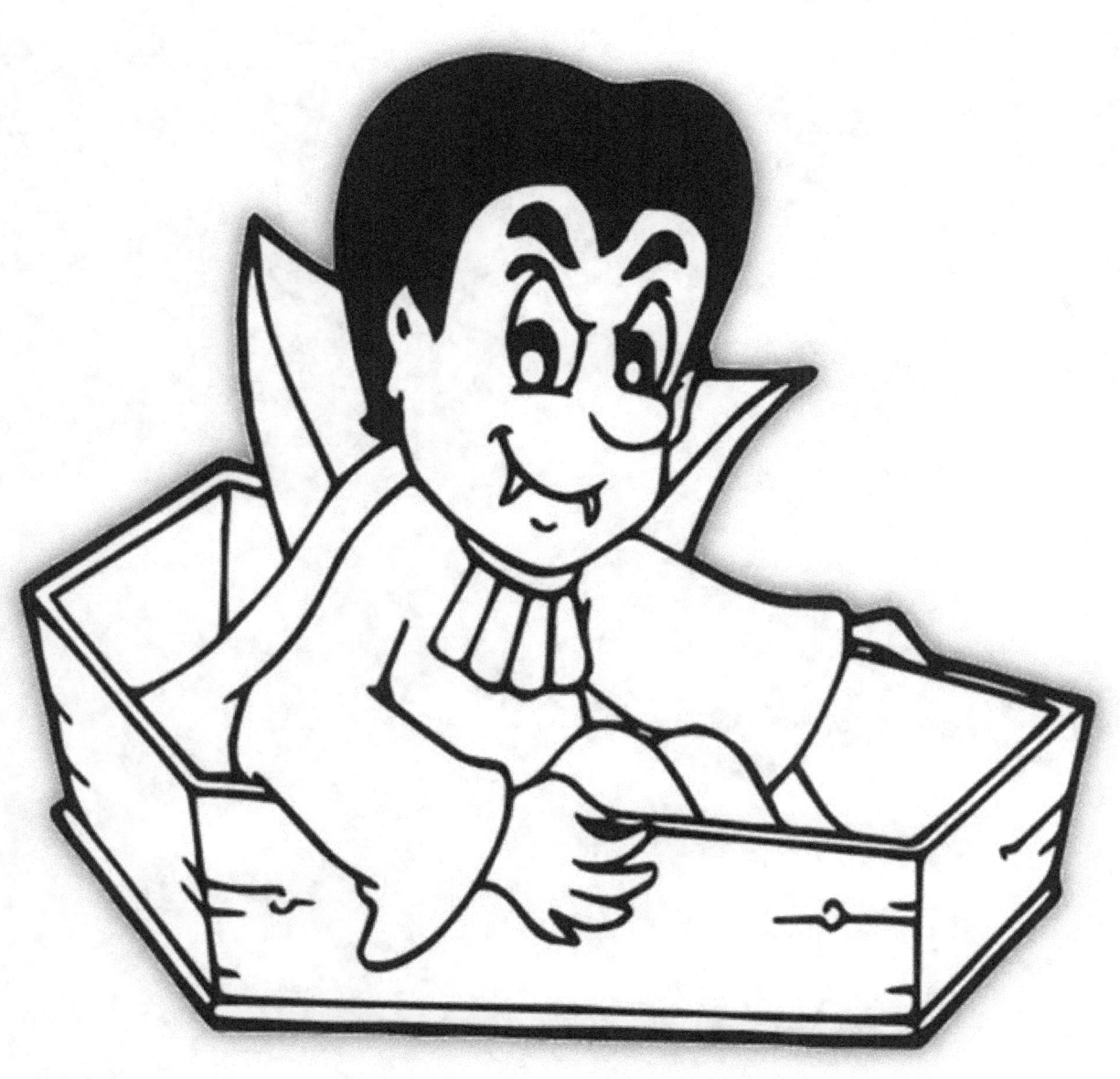

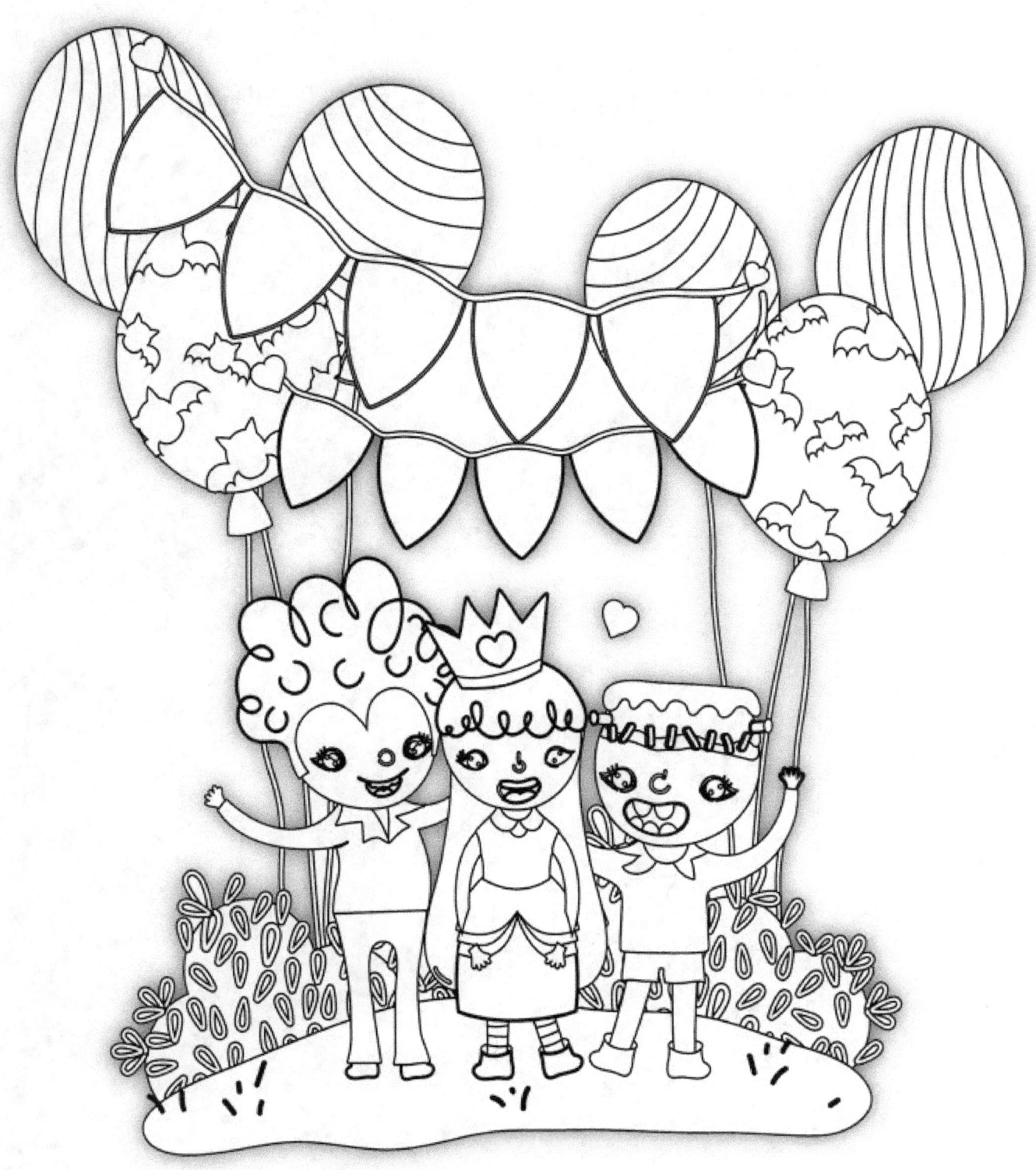

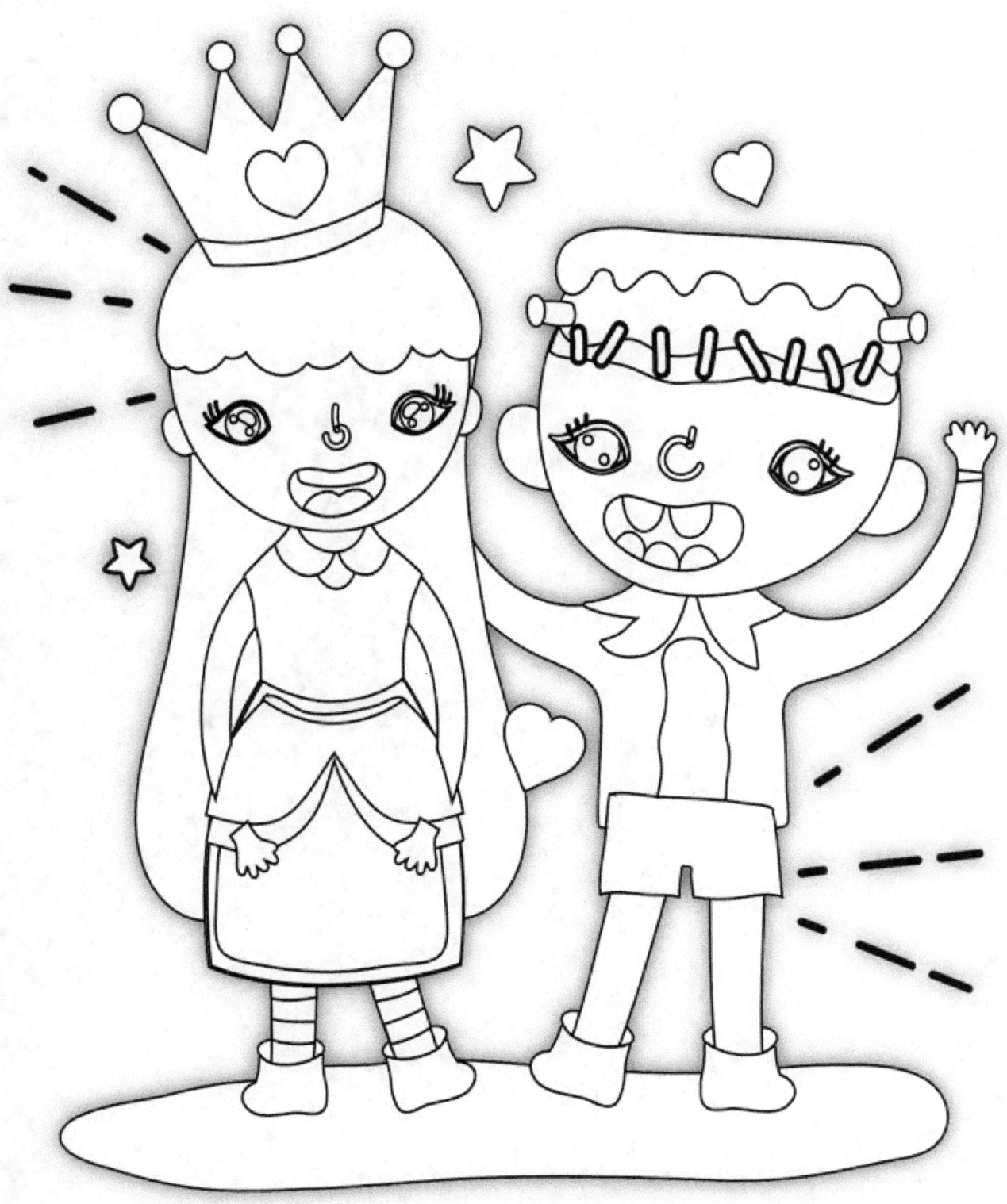

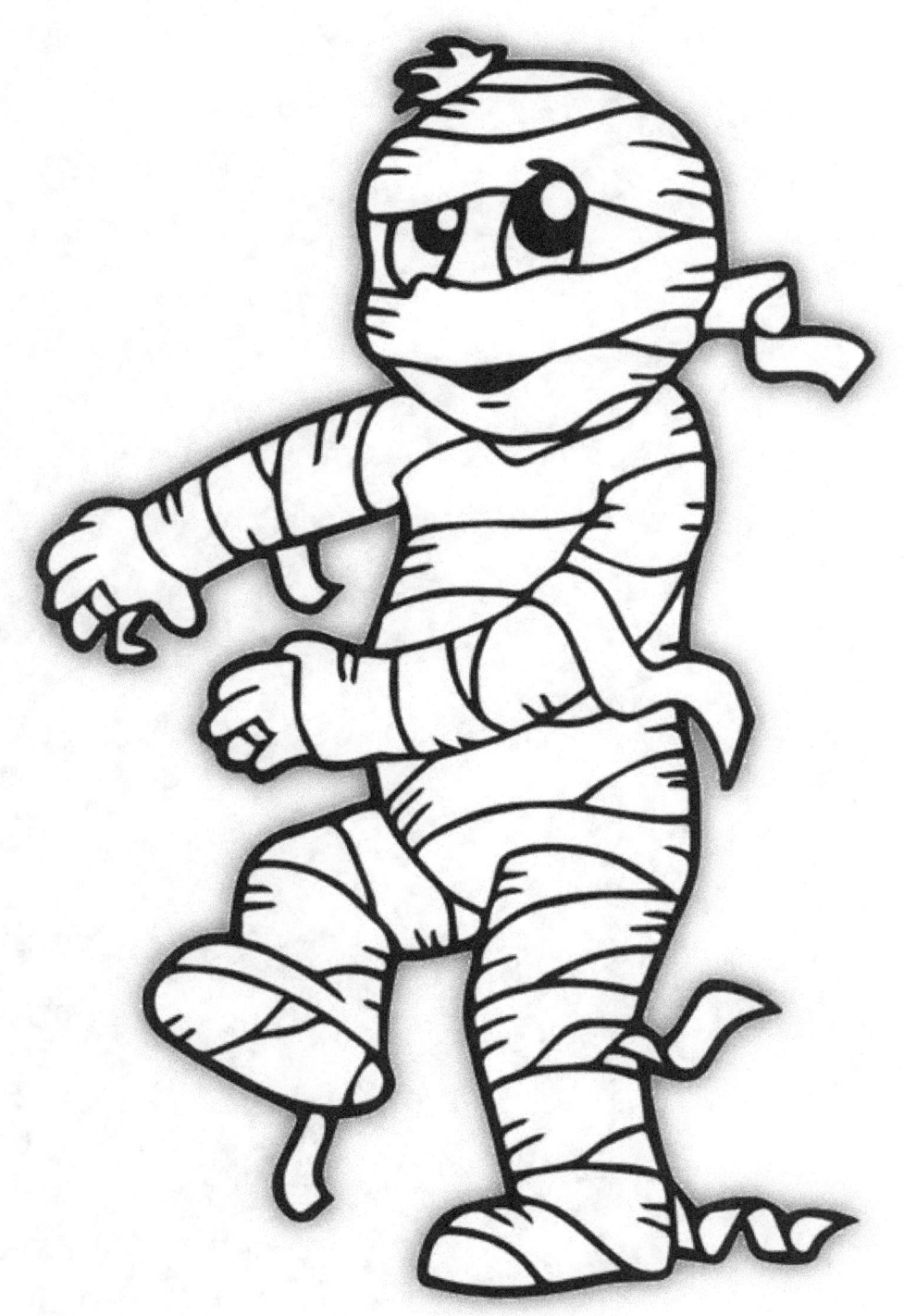

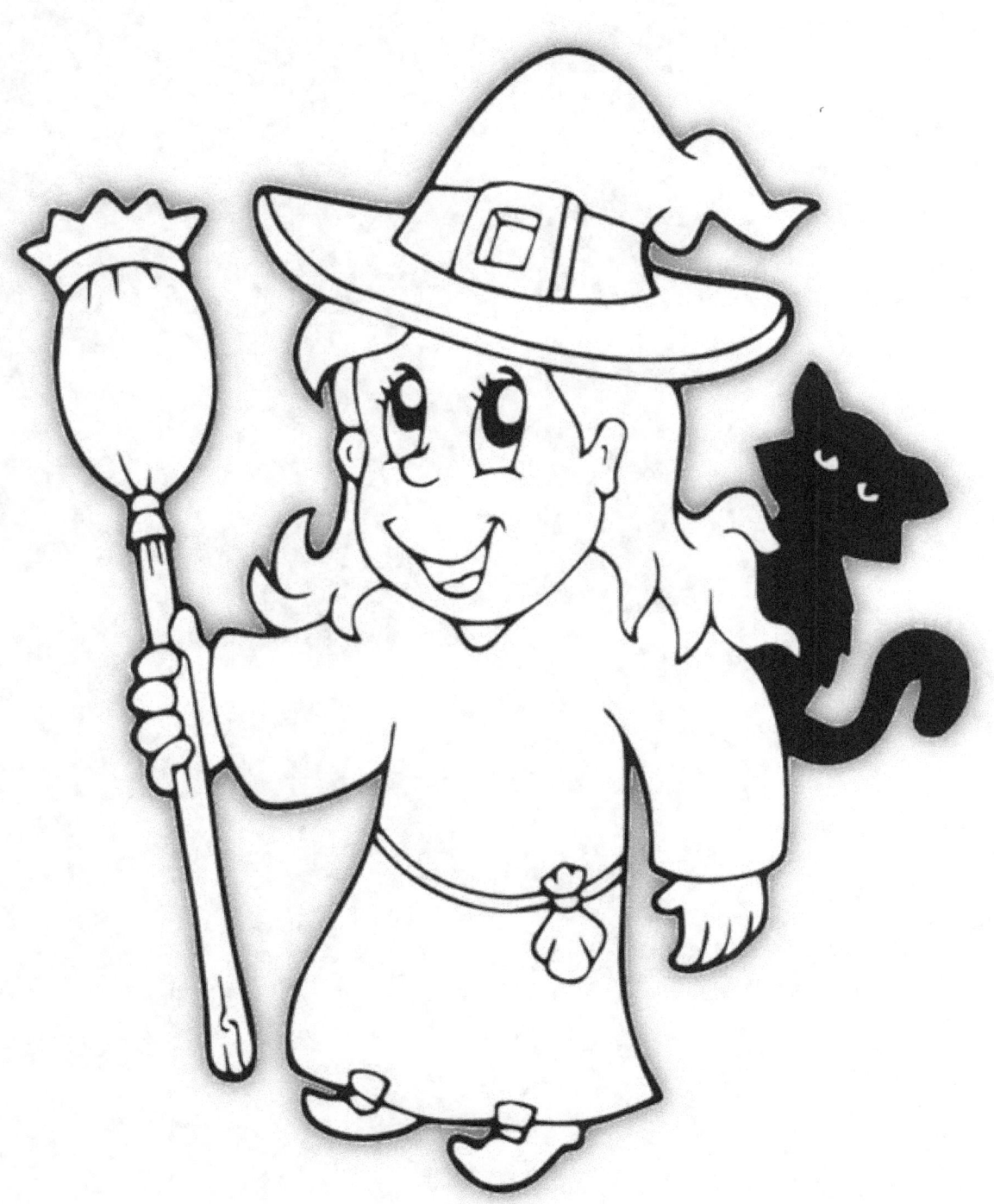

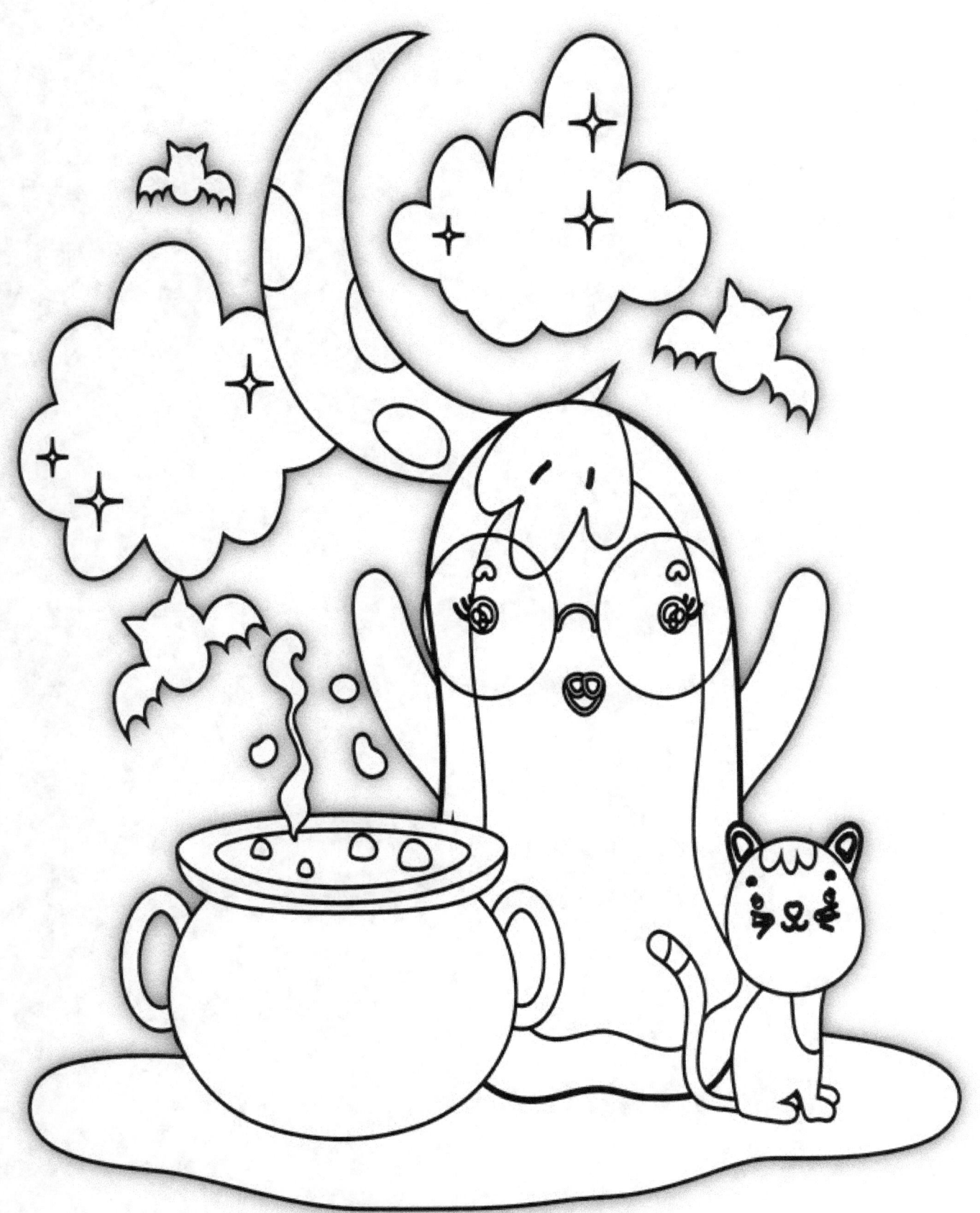

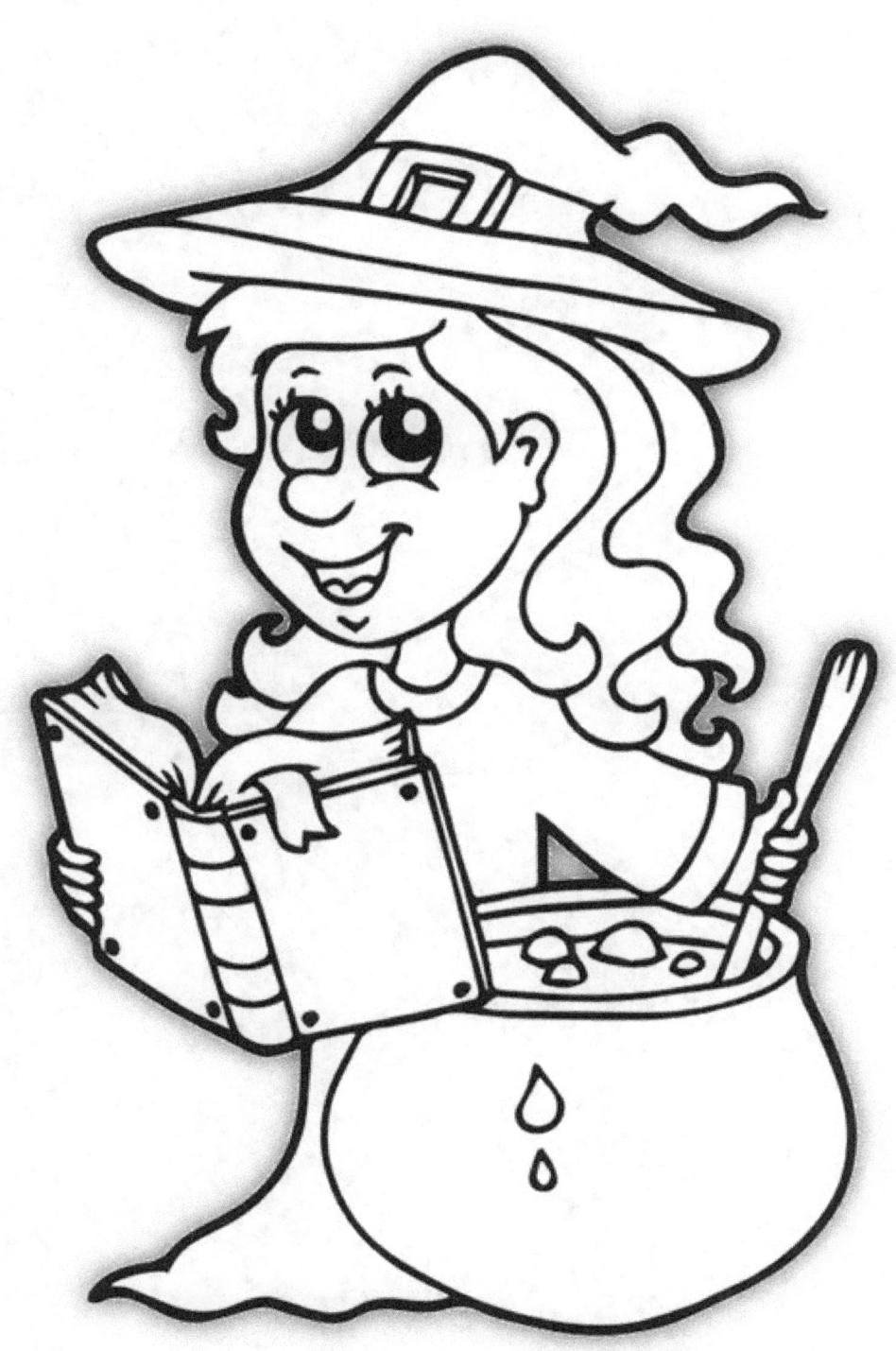

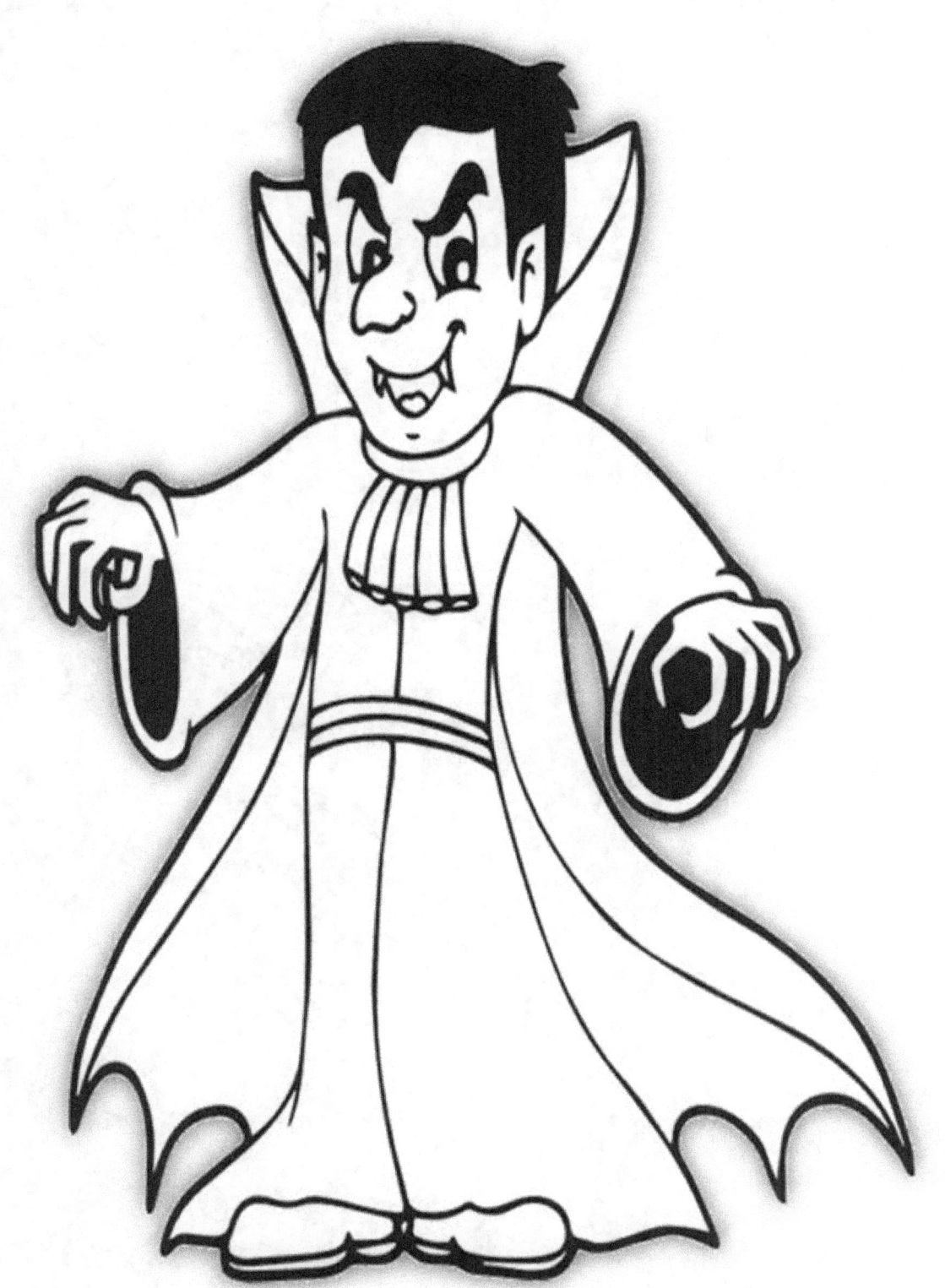

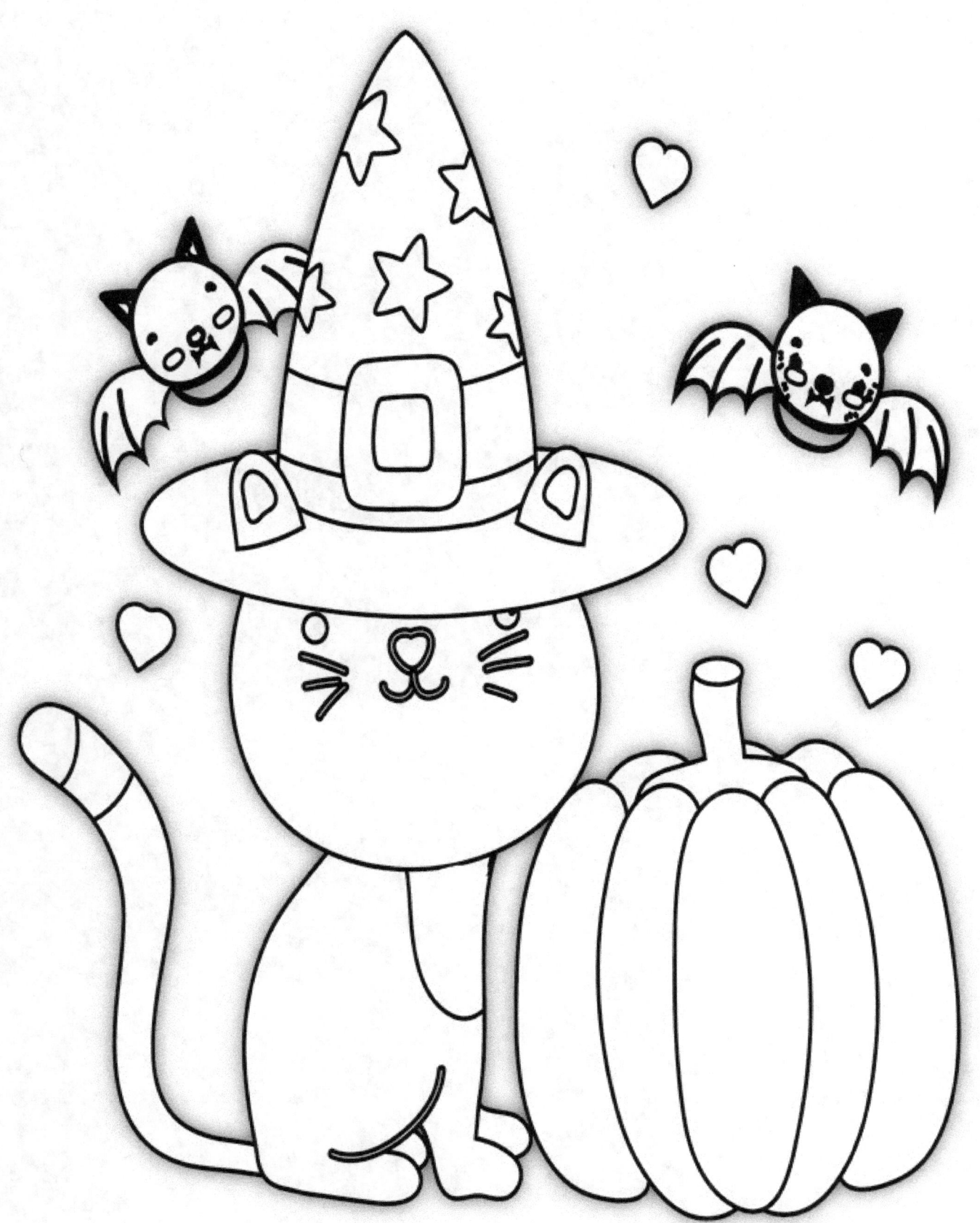

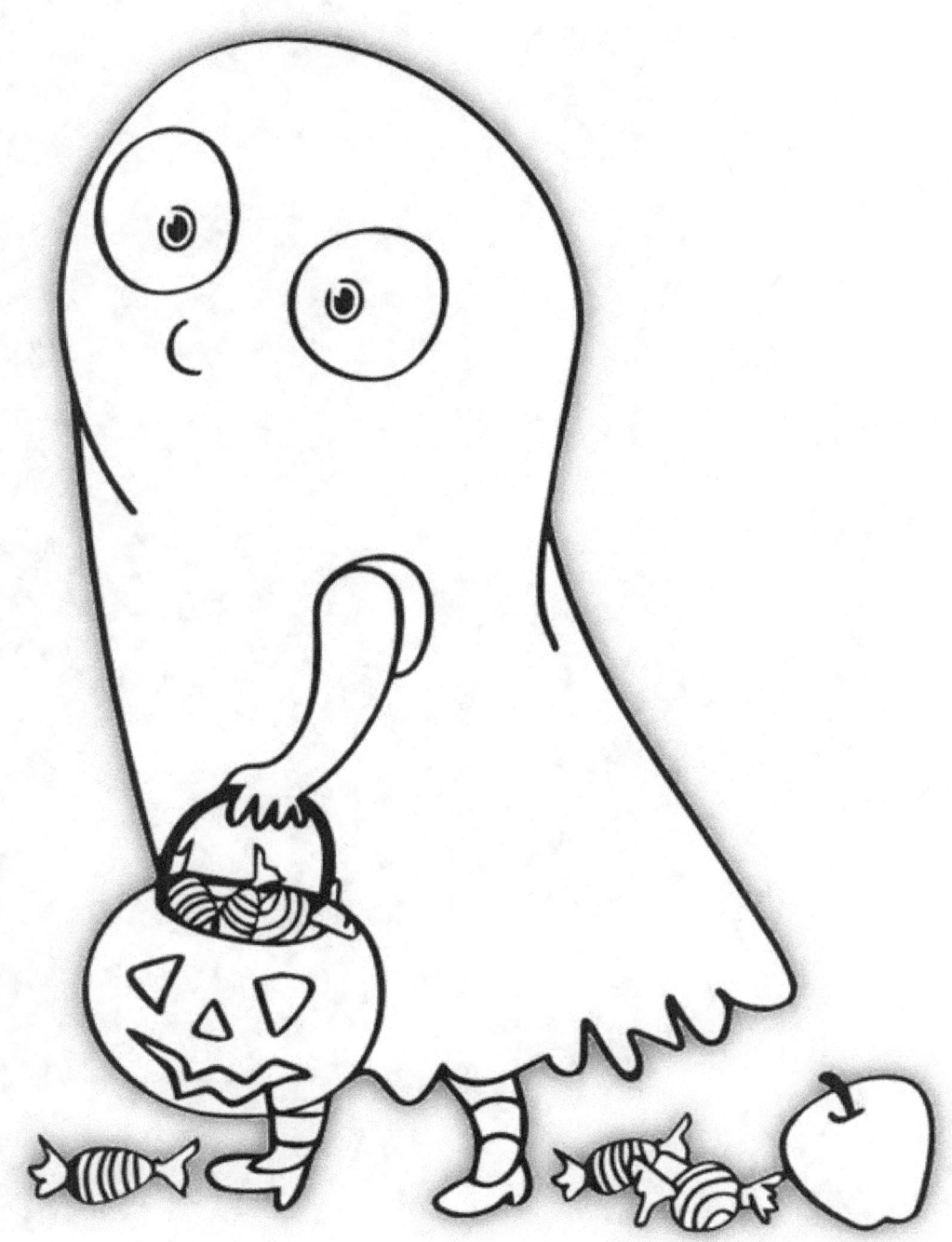